PRINCIPLES OF INVESTING

PRINCIPLES OF INVESTING

A Complete Introduction to
Stock Ownership, Basic Valuation,
and Risk Assessment

FIRST EDITION

By

ADAM LOVE

GARDEN ROAD PUBLISHING
CANADA

Principles of Investing
Copyright © 2013 by Adam Love

Cover artwork and design by Corbyn Knight

www.principlesofinvestingbook.com

Garden Road Publishing, Canada
ISBN-13 978-0-9919300-0-5

First Edition

Dedicated to my family—more important
than any investment.

And to Emily.

Contents

Preface

Growing up, I discovered a natural interest in science and engineering. Few things were more satisfying than designing, building, or simply imagining something mechanical or electronic. The fascination persisted, and to be sure this is what I enjoy doing today. At the same time, my understanding of business and finance was limited at best. If anything, these were subjects that I tended to avoid. I was completely unfamiliar with hedge funds, and the world of investment banking. It was only during my undergraduate years that I came to realize that these were indeed very competitive, very lucrative fields. I was quite surprised when I met some individuals pursuing a career in finance, and shocked by the amount of money they could make by doing it.

Now, you're probably wondering how I came to write a book on investing. More importantly, you might be asking yourself why, among the countless books that have already been published on the subject, I felt it necessary to write this one in particular—why this book *needed* to be written. It takes a little bit of history to get from here to there, and so this is where the story begins.

It was October of 2008, and I had just started my master's degree in electrical engineering. Only weeks earlier the United States Government had taken control of Fannie Mae and Freddie Mac, which together owned or guaranteed nearly half of all mortgages in the country. Merrill Lynch was sold to Bank of America, with Lehman Brothers filing for bankruptcy the following day. The world in financial panic. Every day the stock market was hitting new lows, businesses were shutting down, and jobs were being lost. I will confess that as a student at that time, I felt immune to these events. Academic life seems to have that effect. I knew that I still had two years of school remaining to complete my degree—surely the economy would be running full steam by then.

Even then, every time the stock market dropped, it caught my attention. Like a train wreck, the financial crisis was something you couldn't help but watch. I didn't understand how the stock market worked, or what drove share prices, but I couldn't help but *feel* like the panic couldn't go on forever. At some point, the gloom must end, and things would return to normal, right? Naïve and unaware of the risks, I thought to myself that now might be the time to invest. Instilled with a youthful sense that I had nothing to lose, I decided to open a self-directed investing account through my bank.

I purchased a few thousand dollars' worth of shares in three companies that had a low P/B (price-to-book) ratio, based on my limited understanding of investing at the time. To make a long story short, my investment tripled in three months. I sold my shares and used that money for school. Suddenly investing became a lot more interesting.[1]

I was under no illusion that most of what had just happened was anything but a combination of good luck and timing, probably difficult to repeat, and certainly not to be taken for granted. I wasn't terribly familiar with solvency, liquidity, or cash flow—things I should have understood and taken into consideration given the nature of the economy at the time. I cannot claim to have been completely ignorant. As an undergraduate student, I had been exposed to a mandatory business course—something I have come to value since—but I had only a basic grasp of financial statements on which to screen my investments.

Recognizing this void, I committed much of my spare time to developing my investing knowledge. Like many new investors, I read a number of books, and studied numerous financial statements, to the point that I could quickly and comfortably assess a business's overall financial position. I understood where to find information and how to interpret it. Ultimately, I came to adopt a value-investing strategy. This is probably because it seemed to best reflect many of the very real opportunities that had presented themselves during the financial crisis. This provided me with an approach to investing that was far more rational and concrete than what I had used during my first adventure in the stock market.

Now, this period of learning wasn't as straightforward as I had anticipated. Where I expected to find a clear, unified

---

[1] At the time, it was not unusual to find companies trading for a fraction of their book value. One of those companies went bankrupt less than a year later, even though my investment in that company more than doubled. Looking back, the warning signs were there. Markets can be irrational, and I just got lucky.

consensus for how to approach valuation and risk, I was instead met with a wealth of interpretations and strategies. Some were clear and rational, and others highly questionable. In particular, I came across a lot of references to "technical analysis"—a very popular approach to investing that focuses on price and volume charts in an attempt to determine what share prices will be in the future. This method of picking stocks does not examine a company's financial health directly, and so financial literacy is not a prerequisite. With a strong background in math, and specializing in digital signal processing, I thought that I might be well suited to this approach. To my surprise, this wasn't the case.

The closer I looked, the more skeptical I became of many of these techniques. Most of these approaches centered on identifying trends and analyzing simple moving averages. Given the inherent irrationality and inefficiencies that one can clearly see occurring between market price and fundamentals, trends are one of the most misleading indicators an investor can look at in the short term. Furthermore, to omit any financial valuation in favor of such an analysis seriously concerned me.

If I wanted to be *really* technical, I could write a simple prediction algorithm and apply it to a price chart. These algorithms are powerful; here you have a set of equations that attempt to predict the movements of a seemingly random process by modeling its underlying behavior. This is something of great use in a number of technical applications, but completely ill-suited to the stock market, because stock price is not governed by an equation or a distribution or even a set of distributions. While you can model just about any set of observations as if it were a sum of random processes, and attempt to predict a set of future outcomes based on that model, it would be foolish to blindly accept the results in every application. It's easy to apply any number of mathematically rigorous signal analyses or statistical models to any signal (stock prices included), but that doesn't make the results any more valid or meaningful. This is something that is easily lost in translation when mathematical techniques are applied to fields for which they were never intended. This is particularly true of the stock market.

Many of these approaches, while appearing scientific, seemed to be anything but concrete, and instead made the world of investing more abstract and more distant; a far cry from anything that could be described in clear and practical terms. This did not sit well with me. I believe that it's important to understand *how* something works—the underlying principles—and the stock market was no exception. I felt that the confidence with which many traders and analysts spoke of trend lines, levels of support, and resistance was not terribly useful, was given far too much weight, and was rarely questioned. To claim that you can interpret market sentiment in the short term is only true insofar as you can say that the stock price has gone up or gone down. Beyond that, any interpretation of stock prices is highly questionable.

In a sense, I realized that investing was nothing like math and engineering. It relied on a different analytical approach; one based not on complex calculations to generate new numbers, but on understanding and weighing the numbers you are given. I think it's this appreciation for the differences between math and engineering, and investing that resonated with me, and has been a big part of my motivation for writing this book.

Now, lower your pitchforks and hear me out before you burn this book and declare it a fraud. It's true that many people feel very strongly about the importance of technical analysis. Large financial institutions and funds do hire people who are exclusively focused on technical indicators. Others maintain that both serve some useful purpose, in that fundamental analysis is important for long-term investing, and technical analysis can help you to identify when to buy or sell in the short term. While some people share my opinion of technical analysis, others do not. I want to make that clear. I would encourage you to come to your own conclusions about its validity and importance. You will not find any information on technical analysis in this book. The good news is that the fundamental approaches that are the focus of this book will provide you with a much deeper understanding of stock ownership and valuation—what you're buying—whether you chose to incorporate technical indicators into your investment decision making or not.

Stepping back, if one were to survey many popular books on investing, one would find that a significant number written by "high-profile traders" spend a considerable amount of time talking about the "trading lifestyle." The authors describe "entry points," and discuss "the discipline of having an exit strategy," building excitement in the reader. Some authors will then use this opportunity to promote their trading systems, where you are offered "privileged access" to follow their every trade for "only a modest fee." In most cases these books fail to provide even the most basic understanding of how to assess a company's financial health—how to understand *what* you're buying. Most investors would find much better value taking an introductory college or continuing education course on basic financial analysis. If you haven't already, this is something that I would encourage you to do.

With that said, many of the resources that *did* cover useful information often lacked a clear explanation for the stock market, or a more tangible justification for what drove share prices beyond supply and demand. In many cases they focused on higher-level qualitative principles, without providing a clear overview of the relevant quantitative and financial variables.

For these reasons, I was determined to write a book that covered the fundamental principles of investing in a clear and precise way. It is by understanding these principles that the mysteries have been replaced with a stronger understanding of the risks and opportunities, and I believe a less mysterious stock market is incredibly important for any investor. I have tried to make this book as clear and sensible as possible. I hope that you will find it valuable, and that it will clear up some of the mysteries for you as well.

For those who do choose to invest, never feel rushed. The stock market is a dynamic place, sometimes taking and sometimes creating opportunities for investors. Take your time to understand as much as you can. Without a clear understanding, it certainly can seem overwhelming, or even impossible to invest with any chance of success. Strive to simplify concepts where possible to the point that they become obvious, and try to recognize those situations where there may be risk factors that you do not fully comprehend—something one comes to appreciate the more experience they have. Where you are uncertain, and especially if you are investing large sums of money, you should consider asking an investment professional for his or her opinion.

I firmly believe that knowledge and education have, more than anything, the greatest potential to enable people, and so I hope that this book helps to enable you. Be diligent, be patient, and always try to be aware of the risks. Exercise caution with the amount of capital you allocate to any investment.

While it has been my intent to provide a clear description of all the concepts in this book, some readers might still find certain parts unclear. For this reason, you will find a link to a website at the end of the book where you can contact me to provide feedback, or if you have any outstanding questions that you feel the book did not address. This feedback is important and will be incorporated into future editions.

Thank you to my friends and family for their involvement and feedback—many of their suggestions have had a clear impact on what follows.

Introduction

To many people the stock market might appear to have a mind of its own. In the short term this is a perfectly valid interpretation. *Nobody* can predict with certainty what tomorrow's stock prices will be—this would require prior knowledge of the decisions other investors are going to make. Some maintain that it's nothing more than a high-stakes casino, and that you would have just as much luck taking your money to the slots. Others call it a financial bellwether for the global economic climate; a significantly more compelling, but equally volatile, characterization following every cycle, every crash, and every beat. One day markets are up, the next they're down, inspiring sensationalism and topping headlines. For every change in price, you can expect to find any number of different explanations and opinions. Where some see certain opportunity and throw caution to the wind, others remain skeptical and carefully observe.

For all of the interpretations, uncertainties, and even suspicions, investing in the stock market has never been more accessible. It's not unusual to see discount brokerages and banks marketing directly to the general public. Just about anybody can open a self-directed investment account with ease, and initiate buy and sell orders in real time at his or her convenience. All you need is a little bit of money, a computer, and an Internet connection. Electronic brokers will gladly execute your order regardless of age or experience for a modest fee.

Unfortunately, gains in investment education have not matched the ease and accessibility with which you can now buy and sell shares; few educational institutions have placed any emphasis on financial literacy. While just about anybody can tell you stock prices using a computer or smartphone, only a small minority can clearly describe why the stock market exists, the variables behind share price, or how to make good investment decisions. As a result, many people have jumped in headfirst without any investment background based on news, rumor, or simply on good faith that their stocks will provide a positive return over time. This represents an enormous financial risk, and for many investors should signal that it's time to do some honest homework before putting more of their hard-earned money in the market and hoping for the best. By understanding even the most basic principles behind investing, an investor can begin to recognize and minimize this risk.

When it comes to unraveling the mystery, most books will stop short of explaining what the stock market actually is. Instead, they dive into techniques for making money, whether they work or not, often by using complicated-looking price charts with a few statistical indicators thrown in to lend some credibility to the seemingly esoteric world of stock picking. They might even go a step further by offering a turnkey "trading system," which promises to do all the hard work for you; a blind recipe for what are reportedly certain profits. Many of these techniques attempt to predict where the stock price is going based on historical price and volume patterns alone, and equate to "buy when the market is going up, sell when it's going down"; an investment philosophy that leaves the investor at the mercy of the short-term market, and without any practical financial understanding. Many traders swear by these approaches without once taking the time to learn how to read a balance sheet or income statement.

Price movements are personified and patterns are classified, adding yet another layer of unnecessary complexity and misleading abstraction. This process of cataloging, analyzing, and trying to predict patterns is very human, but the simple fact is that price charts tell you nothing about the value of what you are buying.[2] Just as some people will try to choose "good" lottery numbers, when in fact the sequence *1, 2, 3, 4, 5, 6* is just as likely to be drawn as *5, 13, 22, 37, 39, 48*, patterns can lure investors into a false sense of confidence, putting them at great risk.

It's unfortunate that the level of complexity found in many of these techniques seems only to have added credibility in the eyes of many investors. Bright, technical minds are easily drawn to the study of price patterns, while missing the most important principles on which to make good investment decisions. You don't need calculus or differential equations to invest in stocks. In fact, those are probably the last thing you need. Investing is more about *understanding* the numbers than

---

[2] It is the author's opinion that technical analysis, though widely accepted among many investors and traders, should never form the basis of any investment decision. The reader is encouraged to come to their own conclusion.

calculating them; in most cases basic algebra will more than suffice.

With all this focus on trading and prices, many people would be hard-pressed to describe in any tangible terms what exactly they are buying. Some traders will say, "It doesn't matter, as long as I'm making money" —a simple statement of confidence that can carry a very high price. For most people, however, it might be because the whole notion of the stock market can seem very abstract. When you own only a small fraction of the outstanding shares of a very large company, it can be difficult to believe that you own anything at all. Certainly, the money is real, and you can see the returns or losses over time, but the mechanisms don't necessarily feel transparent. Some believe that shares have value only because it is accepted among other shareholders that there must be, and not because there actually is. This is a common fallacy that fails to consider the very tangible meaning of equity ownership.

It's no surprise that so many investors then fail to recognize the obvious when it comes to fundamentally undervalued or overvalued businesses. Indeed, it's no wonder the stock market is often seen as little more than another casino. The behavior of many investors and traders alike could quite accurately be likened to gambling. With the uncertainty of not knowing what they are buying, they find themselves on the verge of selling almost immediately after purchasing shares.

The simple truth is that the most successful investors have achieved their wealth not by looking at price charts, but by first understanding that you can attempt to determine the value of the underlying business through careful financial and qualitative analysis, and then choosing whether or not to pay the price somebody is offering for a piece of that company. The time-invariant nature of the market is not the outcome of some hidden process, but rather the result of the prices a few people are willing to pay for a portion of various businesses from one moment to another; these businesses hold very real assets that may or may not generate value or earnings for shareholders over the longer term.

So where do you start? How do you look beyond stock price? How do you determine value? This book provides an opportunity to learn the fundamentals in a clear and coherent way. You might be surprised by the information that is available, and what it can tell you.

Chapter 1 begins by clarifying what the stock market is, and the role it plays in very tangible terms—something that is taken for granted, avoided, or in some cases even denied. By the end this chapter, the reader should understand the difference between employees and executives *controlling* a company's assets on behalf of shareholders, and shareholders *owning* the equity of that company.

Chapter 2 introduces the reader to the difference between share price and share value, arguably the most important distinction to be made. This follows a slightly unconventional format, by using an analytical approach that breaks market capitalization down into tangible book value and what we will call speculative value.

Chapter 3 provides a basic introduction to the three principal financial statements—their relevance, and what each of their entries means. Financial accounting can be very complex, but you don't need to be an accountant to understand the most important items.

Chapter 4 focuses on a number of common financial ratios and metrics, useful for interpreting and comparing the information provided in Chapter 3. This chapter also introduces the reader to net present value (NPV), which is useful for estimating the value of a project that a company might choose to undertake. This is especially important for resource and mining companies, which develop and operate complex assets that have varying capital and operational costs over limited lifetimes.

Chapter 5 steps back to provide the reader with a better understanding of how to identify and value a business. This chapter provides a general framework for analyzing a company's financial position, by describing the process that an investor might follow.

Chapter 6 broadens the scope of risk, familiarizing readers with risks that might not be immediately obvious.

Chapter 7 introduces mutual funds and ETFs, highlighting their differences, and describing how units in these funds are created. Most investors should consider investing in a diversified fund.

Chapter 8 covers the common buy and sell orders, and explains in which situations they are appropriate.

At the end of each chapter, you will find a summary of the key principles that have been introduced. You will also find a glossary at the end of this book, which should be helpful if you are unfamiliar with certain financial and investing terms.

If it is your first time reading this book, it is recommended that you begin by reading from front to back, with the exception of Chapter 3, which can be referenced at any time. Because this book emphasizes the use of common financial terminology almost immediately, some terms will be introduced before they are formally defined, but their meaning should be clear from the context in which they are used.

The good news is that these concepts are not that difficult, and there are some excellent resources to help get you started. Of course, no one book will make you a great investor. That's not a disclaimer, it's a fact—books can provide you with very useful background, but every investment is unique and will ultimately require you to make decisions by using a lot of different information under circumstances that are subject to change. Like anything worthwhile, it will require some time and some effort. This book can tell you what a lot of important financial numbers mean and give you some perspective on them, but you will need to do your own homework when it comes to getting a feel for them.

Unfortunately, there are many bad resources that can and will do quite the opposite. While the Internet has made lots of good information more accessible than ever, it has also become a medium for dispersing misleading or even false information on an immediate and unprecedented scale. Many stock forums are saturated with incorrect information, and the novice investor is at the greatest risk. When it comes to investing information and financial advice, question everything you read. Never take anything for granted—if it doesn't make sense, there might be a good reason why.

While this book tries to provide you with a lot of useful information, it should only form a part of your understanding. The author strongly encourages you to take a classroom-based college or continuing education course in basic financial analysis and to supplement this material where you feel you require a better understanding.

Finally, expect to make mistakes! *Everybody* makes them, and investing is certainly no exception. Always do your best to understand what you are buying, and never invest more than you are prepared to lose.

1

The Stock Market

The stock market is a public *equity*[3] marketplace where shares in listed companies can be bought and sold between investors. Shares grant the holder the transferable right to a portion of the equity of a company — equity which is subject to change over time.

In practice, there are actually multiple exchanges where these trades take place, including the New York Stock Exchange (NYSE) in the United States, the Toronto Stock Exchange (TSX) in Canada, and the London Stock Exchange (LSE) in the United Kingdom. These exchanges are in turn owned and/or operated by other companies. In fact, it's not unusual for a company that operates a stock exchange to also be listed on that exchange. For example, in the United States, the NASDAQ OMX Group Inc. operates the NASDAQ

---

[3] Equity is the residual claim on a company's assets after all outstanding liabilities on those assets are paid for, or the portion of the assets that is owned and not just controlled (*see glossary*).

exchange, and is traded under the ticker NDAQ. In Canada, the TMX Group Inc. operates the TSX, while also being traded under the ticker X. Companies that operate these exchanges make money through listing fees, and by selling market data to individuals and investment firms.

Each exchange usually lists different stocks based on region and/or industry. For example, many American companies listed on the NYSE are not traded on the TSX. However, there are exceptions; a company is not prevented from listing on multiple exchanges (cross-listing). In these cases, shares on different exchanges are limited to those exchanges, but tend to trade at similar prices after currency conversion.

Different exchanges may also have different rules and regulations when it comes to meeting listing requirements and trading activity. For example, the proposed Aequitas exchange, scheduled to launch in Canada in 2014 plans to limit high-frequency trading. Governments will usually impose some of their own financial regulations as well.

While these exchanges may have physical locations, one must open an investing account through his or her bank or a brokerage firm, and execute buy or sell orders online or by phone to buy or sell shares directly.

Why Invest In Stocks?

Investing in stocks can be a great way to grow your net worth, and because of the way the market is distributed, there are plenty of ways to do it. There are many different companies that you can own a part of. It's all about understanding and weighing the risks in relation to your expectations and purpose for investing in the first place. Investing in stocks may not be for everybody, and in few cases will it actually replace the income you generate through employment, but for many people it can be a good way to grow your money. If you have outstanding debts, it is probably a better idea to pay those down prior to investing.

Some people like to divide their investments, where most will be allocated to more conservative funds for retirement, and a smaller amount will be invested in a mix of stocks in the hopes of identifying undervalued opportunities. For most people, this is a good approach. For others, the objective of investing is to preserve wealth rather than to grow it, something equally important, with its own unique approaches and challenges.

One commonly held belief is that the stock market is reserved for wealthy participants only. This couldn't be further from the truth. There is no significant financial barrier to participating. If anything, education and understanding are the greatest obstacles to becoming involved. While the level of starting capital varies from individual to individual, every investor has the same opportunity, and access to the same financial information.[4]

In fact, the stock market serves as one of the *most* effective means of achieving something so often advocated by those most opposed to its very existence: distributed ownership. Whereas a small group of individuals might previously have laid claim to the equity of a large business, tens of thousands, if not more, can own a stake instead. You

---

[4] Excluding cases of securities fraud, which do occur, and will certainly continue to exist.

don't have to be Bill Gates to own a part of Microsoft. This is an incredibly powerful concept.

Public and Private Companies

When it comes to investing, there are two sorts of companies: those that trade on the stock market, and those that do not, referred to as being "public" or "private," respectively.[5]

If a company is private, it means that one or more individuals have full rights and ownership to the earnings and equity of that company. You cannot buy shares in privately owned companies on the stock market. Ownership can only be transferred in a private sale. These companies are not required to disclose any financial information to the general public. Private companies can become public in the future.

Many other companies have issued shares that can be traded on the stock market. These companies are referred to as being "public," where the initial public offering (IPO) of shares to investors is a process often referred to as "going public." Shares can be issued one or more times, and subsequently traded between investors on the stock market, where each share represents an equity stake in the company. Public companies can return to being private if all shares are repurchased.

Just about any individual can buy or sell shares in a public company. This is why we call the stock market a *public* equity marketplace. Private companies have equity too, but

---

[5] "Public" companies in this case should not be confused with government-owned corporations.

you cannot buy or sell that equity on the stock market. Public companies are also required to disclose their earnings, assets, and liabilities, among other financial information, to the general public. This information is typically reported every three months (quarterly), to meet listing requirements, though a company may provide additional news and guidance on a more regular basis of their choosing.

Public companies will usually have a section of their website dedicated to investors. Here you can expect to find general information about the company, financial statements, and other documents and presentations, which highlight the past performance and direction of the company using both quantitative and qualitative information. This information is available to everybody, and not just shareholders. Financial transparency is extremely important; it provides insight into the financial health and profitability of a company. It is this financial information that investors should first seek when trying to determine whether an investment is a good idea or not.

Finally, public companies require insiders (senior executives and members of the board of directors) to report when they buy or sell shares in the company.[6] This may or may not be an indicator of the health of the company; many large companies use automatic disposition plans on a regular basis to sell shares held by executives as a means of compensation, irrespective of company performance or share price. For this reason, an investor would be wise to investigate whether such activity is unusual or not.

---

[6] Not to be confused with the illegal form of "insider trading," where third parties buy and sell shares using material information that has not yet been disclosed to the public.

Issuing Shares

One of the first questions you might ask is, "Why have some companies gone public while others have not?" The most common reason is to raise money. All companies require cash[7] at some point to expand, maintain operations, or pay down debt. There are several ways to obtain this cash; they can use their existing cash from previous profits, or even borrow money from the bank, through a loan, if they are approved. In the latter case, the company will be required to pay back the loan, plus interest. Private companies have access to both of these methods of raising cash. There is another method of raising cash, and this is the primary method with which this book is concerned—that is, issuing stock[8] in exchange for cash.

Companies cannot print money like governments. They can, however, create and issue shares that grant the holder(s) certain transferable entitlements and rights in exchange for cash. Each share entitles the shareholder to an equity stake in the company—fractional ownership. An equity stake may increase in value over the course of a company's operations, and this is the investor's incentive. In turn, the company does not need to pay shareholders back directly, as it would a loan.[9] The caveat is that the former private owner(s) (every company is owned by at least one individual) give(s) up part of their stake in equity. While they were previously entitled to all of

---

[7] In this book (and finance in general) cash is used more casually to refer not only to physical currency, but money in an account as well.

[8] All references to "stocks" and "shares" in this book refer to *common stock*, or ordinary shares—what most people will be investing in.

[9] A company may choose to pay out dividends. However, in most cases, the value of your shares is in your equity stake.

the equity in the company, they receive a portion of the newly created shares in the company instead, which they can sell on the stock market to "cash out" their remaining stake in equity if they so choose. In some cases this is also the *reason* why companies go public—as a means for private equity owners to sell all, or part of their ownership.

The former private equity owners usually hold a very large number of shares, and in some cases maintain a *controlling interest* (more than 50% of the outstanding shares, which can have significance when shareholders vote on a motion).

While the company still *controls* its assets, equity is *owned* by shareholders instead. Employees and senior executives still operate the company, and are paid for their performance on *behalf* of shareholders. Keep in mind that executives, and even employees may also hold shares that entitle them to the same rights and equity as any other shareholder.

Shares can then be traded between investors on the stock market. In the case of very large companies worth billions of dollars, this can be a very good thing. It means that no one individual lays claim to the earnings and equity of a private company; rather, any investor can own a piece.

Of course, while you may have a stake in ownership, most investors will not have a stake large enough to make decisions on how the company is run (though as an owner of common shares you may have some voting rights). The board of directors—a group of people responsible for representing the interests of the shareholders—oversees senior executives, who are responsible for company operations.

Companies can issue as many shares as the board of directors allows to raise more cash. All else held equal, the more shares that exist for that company, the less each share is worth—something called *dilution*. Well-run companies should not need to issue more shares. When shares are first issued, the equity value per share is almost always less than the price per share; investors pay a premium today for the prospect of future value.

Companies can issue shares as a means of raising cash, but also as a form of compensation in place of cash. For example, it is not unusual for senior executives to be granted restricted stock—shares that will be transferred to them if and only if certain conditions are met (financial targets and/or they have been employed for a minimum period of time), or the option to buy shares at a fixed price. The idea is that this can motivate executives to perform at a higher level because they will benefit directly through higher share prices. Of course, nothing is free; issuing more shares does dilute the value held by shareholders.

On the limitation of liability for shareholders, you should know that you can lose no more than your initial investment should a company go bankrupt. Of course, losing your entire investment is not a good thing. This simply means that you are not personally liable for outstanding debts in the company—publicly listed companies must be incorporated, and exist as their own legal entity. Creditors are always paid first, before shareholders. If a company's liabilities exceeds the value of its assets, then creditors will be paid only a fraction of what they are owned, leaving nothing for common shareholders.

Trading Shares

There is an important distinction to be made between issuing and trading shares, which is easily overlooked. Once shares have been issued to investors for cash, those shares can be traded *between* investors for higher or lower prices on the stock market. Investors offer to buy and sell shares based on what they believe those shares will be worth in the future (which may or may not be rational), as a consequence of the company's current financial health, and expected earnings (or losses). In this way, the right to equity ownership is transferred to new shareholders.

These price movements have absolutely no impact on the cash the company had already raised. Therefore, the price chart reflects what some investors have been willing to pay for shares, between themselves, since those shares were first issued. The price at any one instance of time represents the most recent transaction for some fixed volume of shares. For every buyer there must be a seller.

Stock Quotes

Stock quotes provide information about past and present trading activity. Figure 1 shows a sample quote for a fictional company called Precious Metals Mining Corp. with the ticker PRMC.

1 **Precious Metals Mining Corp. (PRMC)**

2 **8.65** + 0.11 (1.29%)

Feb 6, 2013, 12:34pm

3 **Bid/ Size:** 8.64/ 1,000   **Ask/ Size:** 8.65/ 12,000   **4**

5 **Daily Range:**   8.57 – 8.72

6 **52 week Range:**   7.95 – 17.71

7 **Vol/ Avg:**   855,000/1.89M

8 **Mkt Cap:**   3.26B

9 **Shares:**   376M

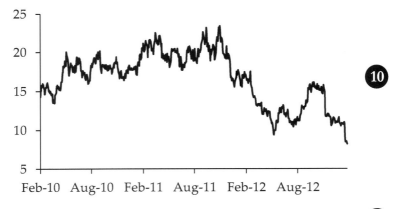

Figure 1: Price information for ticker PRMC

1 The name of the company and ticker symbol. A stock ticker is a short, unique identifier a company uses on each exchange where it is listed.

2 The last trading price, and the time at which the last trade occurred, including the absolute dollar change and the percent change since the start of the day.

3 The highest price (Bid) an investor is willing to pay for shares, and the number of shares sought at that price.

4 The lowest price (Ask) an investor is willing to sell shares for, and the number of shares available at that price.

5 The lowest and highest share prices that day.

6 The lowest and highest share prices over the last year.

7 The number of shares traded today (Vol) and the average number of shares traded daily (Avg).

8 The market capitalization of the company, calculated as the last trading price times the number of shares outstanding.

9 The total number of shares outstanding.

10 The historical price chart.

11 The volume of shares traded.

One number of particular significance is the market capitalization. The market capitalization is calculated by multiplying the most recent share price by the number of shares outstanding. Market capitalization is more important than share price alone, because it accounts for the total number of shares that exist—it gives us the total *market* value of the company (which may or may not fairly reflect the *actual* value of the company—the market isn't always right). Share price in itself is meaningless without knowing how many shares exist. To say that one company is cheaper than another because it has a lower share price is a common fallacy that is fundamentally incorrect.

A common misconception is that market capitalization represents the amount of money that a company could be purchased for—realize that not all investors are willing to sell at the current share price. Many others may prefer to sell at a higher price, and so if you wanted to buy all shares at that price, you would find yourself unable to do so. This is important to understand.

Shares can be traded during normal trading hours on the exchange(s) on which they are compliant with listing requirements.

Investing Principles

- You can buy shares in publicly listed companies, which are required to disclose financial information every quarter. This information is public.

- Private companies "go public" when they issue their first IPO. This is a method of raising cash without having to pay that money back to investors. In exchange, investors are entitled to an equity stake in the company, which may become worth more or less over time—shareholders become the owners.

- While shareholders are entitled to the equity of a public company, the company still controls its assets, and executives and employees are still responsible for running the company on behalf of shareholders—a service for which they are compensated, just like a private company. Some employees and former owners may also be shareholders. The board of directors is responsible for representing the interests of shareholders.

- The price shares are subsequently traded for between investors has no impact on the cash that the company raised when it initially issued them.

- Market capitalization is a measure of how the company is being valued by the market, which accounts for the number of shares outstanding.

2

Price and Value

The distinction between price and value is arguably one of the most important concepts for an investor to understand. The efficient-market hypothesis suggests that all information is known to the market, and that the market has rational expectations. From this, it concludes that share price accurately reflects share value. In other words, given no further news, the efficient-market hypothesis would have you believe that the price you pay is fair value because the market always prices stocks correctly.[10] Some people have even extended this to say that you cannot beat the market, because it would be impossible to buy undervalued stocks. This hypothesis has formed the foundation upon which many investing books have been written.

---

[10] Remember, "the market" can consist of anybody and everybody; some stocks trade between only a handful of buyers and sellers, in limited volumes.

However, there is considerable evidence to suggest that share price and share value are often out of sync. It is now generally accepted that the efficient-market hypothesis is not correct, at least not in its strong form. In practical terms, this means that some very bad companies can trade at substantial premiums, and that some very good companies can trade at substantial discounts to their actual value. That isn't to say that the market is always wrong. There is usually some correlation between price and value, but this should never be taken for granted. We might say that the efficient-market hypothesis is only weakly supported, or that the market is more efficient at pricing certain companies and sectors than others. Never assume that the market price represents fair value. This rules out investing that is strictly qualitative in nature.

It follows that stock price in itself is a meaningless indicator of investment potential, and this extends to historical stock prices as well. To attempt to predict future stock price based on historical prices and volumes alone has been called the financial equivalent of astrology. Even so, there are many investment strategies that attempt to do this, and only this. Some analysts look to historical prices (sometimes over years) as indicators of fair value. When the stock price goes way up, then way down, many assume that there must have been a bubble, and so they will project historical prices. They fail to account for the fact that the equity and cash flow of the underlying business may have been very different at the time of those historical prices. Once a stock price deviates sufficiently from technical expectations, some analysts will even conclude that "the chart is broken," suggesting that they have no idea what the value is.

Recognizing this market inefficiency is important, because it represents an opportunity for investors—both to identify undervalued stocks as potential investments and to recognize overvalued stocks to avoid. Of course, recognizing the existence of this inefficiency is only the first step. The challenge is in identifying those stocks where this inefficiency actually presents itself, and whether or not it is in favor of the investor.

So how do we determine share value? One analytical approach to understanding the difference between price and value is to break share price down into two parts. The first is what is commonly referred to as "tangible book value per share"—an estimate of the equity (in cash) shareholders would receive for each share, if the company sold their tangible assets and paid down all outstanding liabilities today.[11] This is a conservative measure of the liquidation value per share (the value shareholders receive if the company liquidated). The other is what we will call "speculative value per share"—the difference between share price and the tangible book value per share, which can be thought of as the premium or discount on tangible book value per share that investors are willing to pay today based on expected earnings or losses.

Because financial statements tend to report total dollar amounts, rather than per-share amounts, it can be more useful to consider market capitalization directly, rather than share price, when performing any valuation. Consequently, for the purposes of this chapter we will talk about the *total* "tangible book value" and "speculative value."

---

[11] Assuming assets are listed at fair market value on the balance sheet. Depending on accounting rules, some assets (e.g., property) may be listed at their purchase price, which may be higher or lower than their current market value.

Along those lines, if we can accept that the markets at least attempt to be rational, we might call the current market capitalization the *"expected* value," which may or may not be correct. Note that "expected" in this case is an inexact reference to the future; there is no specific date. This is something useful to keep in mind, but for now let's focus on understanding tangible book value and speculative value based on the current market capitalization.

Market Capitalization = Tangible Book Value (Today) + Speculative Value (Future)

While this method of breaking-down market capitalization is unconventional (you probably won't find it described this way in any other books), it is useful because it makes the relationship between price and value clear. In practice, the relationship between market capitalization and tangible book value is usually expressed as a ratio (the P/B ratio, which will be introduced later), where a lower ratio means that you are paying less of a premium on tangible book value (or even a discount, if it is less than one).

Before we continue, it is important to keep in mind that a company has tangible assets (economic resources, including cash, investments, property, inventory, and equipment) and liabilities (money it might owe on some of those assets), with some net equity (the difference between total assets and total liabilities, or the portion of the assets shareholders own) that might be positive or negative at any given time. However, most companies are more complex than a simple sum of assets and liabilities. They may also generate (or lose) cash as a consequence of their operations. As a result, their assets, liabilities, and equity can also change. It follows that tangible book value is rarely fixed. You can calculate tangible book value today, but it can be quite different tomorrow, three months from now, or several years from now—this is what investing in stocks is all about.

Tangible book value can be readily calculated from a company's balance sheet by discounting intangible items[12] from equity (including goodwill), and can be positive or negative. If tangible book value is negative, it means that shareholders would receive nothing if the company liquidated their tangible assets—the money the company owes exceeds the value of its tangible assets. Speculative value is worth only what another perceives it to be worth based on his or her expectations of tangible book value in the future.[13] Speculative value accounts for the possibility that tangible book value can change, and can also be positive or negative depending on investor expectations.

Shares of a company that is expected to make money in the future will typically trade at a premium to tangible book value, whereas shares of a company that is expected to lose money in the future may trade at a discount to tangible book value. Because it tries to price future potential and risk, speculative value is subject to a wide range of interpretations, and accounts for much of the daily price fluctuations you see. The market is not always right, and can be highly irrational.

Many investors will not think of a share price as being composed of these two very distinct components—only share

---

[12] Intangible items are non-physical assets that are recognized to have value on the balance sheet, and include things like brand names and patents.

[13] And in some cases, the value of future dividends as well.

price is reported—but they would benefit from doing so. It helps to know what you are actually paying for once you dismiss the efficient-market hypothesis, and this distinction can help as part of a rational valuation framework. How much of the price you pay for a share represents tangible value today? Is there any? How much is speculative? Does the speculative valuation make sense? At the highest level, this is how you determine whether a stock is a good investment or not—the difference between price and value.

We might then define investing as the process of identifying and purchasing shares in those companies whose speculative value is underestimated by the market, through careful valuation and risk analysis.

Tangible Book Value

While it's one thing to say that you are entitled to some of the equity in a company, it can be quite another to understand what that means. Many people tend to think of a share as having some loose association to a company, which can be bought and sold because it is accepted that it must have value—almost as if the entire stock market operated on some unspoken faith between investors. This is probably one of the main reasons why so many people distrust the stock market.

So, what makes tangible book value *real* for shareholders? In practice, a company could choose to cease operations at any given time, sell its assets, pay off its liabilities, and return the remaining equity in cash to its shareholders (assuming there was something left). Of course, this isn't a decision that you as a shareholder get to make—the company still controls the assets—but if it were in the interest of shareholders, and they agreed to it, nothing would prevent this from happening. Recognizing this gives share ownership a more tangible appeal; there is real value that belongs to you, not simply because it is agreed among investors that there must be. Investors *own* that equity, and it *can* be unlocked. Tangible book value is a conservative estimate of that equity, by discounting goodwill and intangibles, which are arguably speculative. This *is* the link between stocks and companies.

While a company *could* liquidate and pay shareholders the cash value of their equity, a more plausible scenario is that another company (private or public) could purchase the company that you own shares in. If this is the case, it is not uncommon for you to be paid in cash for your shares, at a price above the current tangible book value per share for the same reason that market capitalization is typically higher than tangible book value; this is because a business may be worth more than just the difference between its tangible assets and liabilities. The future profit the business might generate has speculative value, in that while it may not exist now, it could exist in the future. In either case, tangible book value can represent a solid baseline for establishing fair value, today.[14] This mechanism can help to keep markets efficient—whereas shares may trade between investors irrationally, larger players may make cash bids to acquire a company, where they see value that the market does not.

This should make the importance of tangible book value clear—that it has concrete value (which may be zero) and that shareholders are entitled to a portion. It's on the books, and

---

[14] This doesn't mean that any company trading below tangible book value is a good investment. Sometimes there is a good reason for it to trade at a discount.

it's protected by law just like any property you might own in a free-market system.

All of this is well and good to understand, but for the most part, the goal of any company is to be profitable and generate future value, by paying dividends on those profits and/or by growing and accumulating shareholders' equity. For this reason, it is quite uncommon for a company to liquidate and distribute the cash to shareholders.

Some companies can be very well run and profitable but still not expect much growth within their industry. These companies will sometimes pay out most of their quarterly profits in the form of dividends, so the tangible book value may remain fairly unchanged. This runs directly against the common misconception that all companies must grow and accumulate more assets. They can instead maintain the same size and pay out a regular cash flow to shareholders.

Remember, tangible book value and equity are not always the same thing. Tangible book value discounts intangible items from equity to arrive at a more conservative measure of value. Some intangible items can exist on a company's balance sheet, quite possibly overrepresented and overvalued, and may be subject to a write-down, in which case the company will acknowledge this and remove them from the balance sheet.

Finally, companies are run by people, and while these people are charged with treating the interest of shareholders as a top priority, they do sometimes burn through shareholders' equity that may exist today, never to be recovered, and in some cases resulting in bankruptcy. While tangible book value may be very attractive relative to market capitalization today, you cannot be assured that it will be properly managed.

Speculative Value

It is important for investors to understand and be wary of speculative value. While it serves an important purpose, it can also be subject to a high degree of uncertainty. As mentioned earlier, tangible book value is a real thing, based on real assets and real liabilities. Speculative value is the premium or discount on tangible book value that investors pay, because companies are dynamic things, able to make or lose more money over time. This arises both consciously as the result of future expectations, and unconsciously by the free-market nature of the stock market, where investors are free to choose the prices at which they would like to buy or sell stocks (not all investors think of stock price in terms of tangible and speculative components, or think rationally about what they are buying or selling).

Companies where investors expect higher earnings growth tend to trade with a higher speculative value, so we might think of speculative value as being priced as a multiple of expected earnings. Investing in such stocks can be quite a bit riskier. Should operations not transpire as investors had expected, speculative value can drop very quickly, meaning your shares could trade at a much lower price. At the same time, if the company is expected to lose a lot of money, it can also be quite rational for the market capitalization to be below tangible book value, in which case speculative value would be negative. If tangible book value is negative, then the entire share price represents speculative value—your shares may have zero liquidation value today.

Stock market bubbles usually occur when speculative value is priced unreasonably high—when market capitalization exceeds tangible book value (or equity, if you want to be less conservative) by unrealistic multiples. Many people worry about bubbles because of changes in stock prices alone. Investors who take the time to calculate the speculative premium today (simple subtraction) have taken the first step towards understanding and quantifying that risk.

In the case that a company has very predictable operations and cash flow, speculative value should be easier for the market to price. Ultimately, it is up to the investor to decide whether the speculative premium makes sense or not. In most cases, this involves analyzing and estimating future earnings and cash flows.

Finally, it would be naïve not to mention that short-term share price can also be heavily influenced by machine trading—automatic buying and selling—which is driven by algorithms often based on technical metrics. In fact, the majority of trades on some exchanges are performed by computers this way. We can lump this into the less conscious speculative component of market capitalization. While the algorithms might be held as "valuable, closely guarded secrets," these techniques frequently buy when they see lots of buying, and sell when they see lots of selling, or they take advantage of high-speed changes in market orders and depth—something most investors will not see. For the most part, from the perspective of the individual investor, this only serves to amplify volatility. Some exchanges have even had to halt trading because of it.

Investing Principles

- Share price and share value are not always the same thing. Never assume they are.

- Market capitalization represents what investors think the company will be worth in the future. This can be decomposed into tangible book value, and speculative value.

- Tangible book value is a conservative estimate of the liquidation value of a company at the present time, and can be calculated from a company's balance sheet. If the company were to sell all tangible assets, and pay all liabilities, this is the cash that would be generated for shareholders.

- Speculative value represents the premium (or discount) on tangible book value that investors are willing to pay based on future expectations.

- Speculative value is subject to risk and uncertainty, which is what makes investing in stocks and equity unique.

- Stock market bubbles are often characterized by unrealistically high speculative value—something investors can calculate.

- Both tangible and speculative value can be positive or negative.

3

Financial Statements

There are three principal financial statements, and before you invest you must have a strong understanding of each. These statements are the balance sheet, the income statement, and the cash flow statement. They provide insight into the financial health and profitability of a business. This is also where you will find the tangible book value, discussed in the previous chapter. Financial statements are generally standardized, and so the items and their presentation should be familiar between companies. There are several different accounting standards that are followed, including the Generally Accepted Accounting Principles (GAAP) in the United States, and the International Financial Reporting Standards (IFRS) used by most of the world.[15]

---

[15] Many countries are moving to adopt IFRS accounting standards. In 2011, companies listed on the TSX were required to switch to IFRS to meet listing requirements.

The first step to being able to read and understand these statements is to familiarize yourself with the definitions of each of their items—what do the numbers mean? This is something that this chapter can help you with. The second step involves some practical experience. Try to familiarize yourself with financial statements from different companies to have some idea of the ranges of reported values. You should be able to place a company's financial health in relation to the normal range when compared to its peers and other publicly listed companies. While there is a bit of a jump between these two steps, it can be accomplished with some motivation, time, and patience. That jump will never be automatic.

These statements are typically reported once every quarter, and summarized every year to meet regulatory listing requirements. Depending on the exchange, there may be several months between the end of a financial quarter and when the financial statements for that quarter are actually reported. This means that the financial information that investors receive is usually a few months behind the company's actual operations. This is important to keep in mind in situations where the company is losing money and is tight on cash.

While most public companies will provide financial results directly on their websites, there are several other places where you can find this information, including the website of the United States Securities and Exchange Commission (SEC) for American companies, and SEDAR in Canada. Third-party financial websites like Google Finance or Yahoo Finance also try to aggregate this information along with relevant news. While third-party websites can be very convenient, and certainly easier to navigate, they are sometimes missing certain financial entries and items. Therefore, it is recommended that you should try to find the full set of financial reports before you invest in any company. In general, a company's website is the best place to find this information.

Financial statements are like scorecards, and so most of the numbers you should need are summarized and easy to find. Their standardized format also makes it easy to compare businesses. It's just a matter of knowing *what* you are looking for. This section is written like a study guide, providing you with a high-level description of the major elements that you will usually find in each of the financial statements. While there are some important differences between the GAAP and IFRS accounting standards, most of these differences are beyond the scope of this book, and have been omitted in the interest of clarity while introducing this material.[16]

It is not unusual for some traders to completely ignore financial statements, but they do so at their own risk. Remember, many stocks are priced at significant premiums, and just because the historical price trends look "good" doesn't mean you're buying something that has any value at all. In fact, you could easily be buying shares in a company that loses money, and has no tangible value whatsoever.

---

[16] For a detailed review of financial statements and the differences between GAAP and IFRS accounting rules, the reader is encouraged to review *International Financial Statement Analysis*, by the CFA Institute.

The Balance Sheet

The balance sheet provides a snapshot at a specific moment in time, listing all the assets a company controls (economic resources, including cash, inventory, and property), liabilities (money owed on some, all, or in excess of those assets), and equity (the difference between assets and liabilities, or the portion of the assets that is owned by shareholders). The balance sheet for a fictional company with the stock ticker PRMC is shown in Table 1.

The balance sheet has to balance. That is, for each and every quarter, total assets must equal the sum of total liabilities and total equity. This can be thought of as follows: Assets are anything and everything, tangible and intangible, that a company controls. Those assets are owned by shareholders (equity), and/or funded through debt (liabilities).

$$\text{Total Assets} = \text{Total Liabilities} + \text{Total Equity}$$

In general, most balance sheets will look similar to the one shown in Table 1. There may be a few additional items that are not shown in this example. In this case, those items are lumped under Other Current Assets, Other Long-Term Assets and Other Liabilities.

In Millions of USD	2012	2011	2010
Cash & Equivalents	1,172	317	231
Accounts Receivable	109	55	62
Inventory	239	204	162
Other Current Assets	23	21	21
Total Current Assets	1,543	597	476
Property/Plant/Equipment	3,517	3,280	2,946
Accumulated Depreciation	-1,279	-1,185	-1,107
Goodwill	256	267	334
Intangibles	4	5	8
Long-Term Investments	141	346	248
Other Long-Term Assets	167	121	91
Total Assets	**4,349**	**3,431**	**2,996**
Accounts Payable	339	242	198
Current Portion of LT Debt	-	-	-
Total Current Liabilities	339	242	198
Total Long-Term Debt	0	0	0
Other Liabilities	536	487	358
Total Liabilities	**875**	**729**	**556**
Common Stock	2,309	2,255	2,203
Retained Earnings	1,165	447	237
Total Equity	**3,474**	**2,702**	**2,440**
Total Common Shares Outstanding (in millions)	375	372	368

Table 1: Annual balance sheet for PRMC

Cash & Equivalents

To do business, every company will need (and hopefully generate) cash. Some companies have tens of billions of dollars in cash and equivalents, while others can have much less than they need. The "equivalents" in this case refer to highly liquid, secure, short-term investments that can be converted to cash quickly and easily.

Having a lot of cash can be a good thing, because that cash is readily available to meet expenses or acquire useful assets—a company may not need to borrow money for large expenditures. At the same time, too much cash can be a sign of a poorly managed company, because money sitting in an account doesn't generate a very high return; cash should be deployed to provide a meaningful return on investment.

Sometimes companies will return this cash to shareholders in the form of dividends—unlocking some of their equity—when the company doesn't need that cash to grow.

Accounts Receivable

Accounts receivable lists payment that is owed to the company, which has not yet been collected. Many companies will grant their customers an operating line of credit, and money that is owed to them is accounted for here. This money will usually be collected within a year.

Inventory

Inventory lists the value of finished goods available for sale, and the raw materials used to make those products. While it is important to have sufficient inventory on hand to meet customer demand, pooling too much inventory uses up valuable cash, and may indicate that products are being manufactured but are not being sold. Some inventory can expire, while other manufactured products can become outdated and require disposition at a price that is below manufacturing cost, if it is at all possible.

Total Current Assets

Total current assets is the sum of all cash and equivalents, accounts receivable, inventory, and other current assets. These assets are considered to be current because they can easily be converted to cash within a year — they are liquid. All other assets are considered to be noncurrent or "fixed" because it may be more difficult or impossible to convert them to cash in the same time frame.

Property/Plant/Equipment

Property, plant, and equipment (PPE) are fixed, tangible assets listed at the sum of their purchase price(s). These items can *never* appreciate on the balance sheet even if their market value increases (technically while this is always true under GAAP, IFRS is more flexible, allowing for asset appreciation under certain circumstances[17]). This is an important conservative accounting rule to understand. If some of these assets have appreciated, some companies may indicate that their market value may be higher than what is shown on the balance sheet separately. Appreciation is only recognized

---

[17] For the rest of this book, references to listed asset values on the balance sheet will follow the GAAP convention, as it is more conservative, and still prevalent among most companies in the United States.

indirectly on the sale of those assets, in the sense that the company may be able to sell them for more than their purchase price.

Accumulated Depreciation

Since PPE represents the sum of the total cost of those assets, accumulated depreciation is a negative value that represents the total depreciation of those assets at the current moment in time, relative to their purchase price. This is meant to account for the fact that some assets wear out or lose value over the course of their useful lives.

Goodwill

Goodwill, also known as "cost in excess," represents a special case of accounting, and is subject to the risk of being overvalued on a company's balance sheet. When a company acquires another company, it will typically be paying a premium above the equity of that company—there is usually some unrealized future value, perhaps in customer base, earnings potential, brand, etc. This value is speculative. It has risk, and might not materialize for any number of reasons. Goodwill is a placeholder for that speculative value, the idea being that it must exist or the acquisition wouldn't have taken place at a premium to equity in the first place. This effectively prevents the equity of the acquiring company from dropping when it pays a cash premium in an acquisition.

But sometimes management is wrong. Sometimes the premium on the acquisition had no value. In such a case, goodwill has to be written down, or removed from the balance sheet, which can result in a substantial loss to what was previously reported as shareholders' equity (the balance sheet has to balance).

Always be aware of goodwill. Since this is considered an intangible item, many investors will discount it completely from equity.

Intangibles

Intangibles are assets that are not physical, but which may have some value, such as brand, or intellectual property, including patents. Some of these items can be very difficult to value fairly, and so intangibles are also subject to the risk of overvaluation. Not unlike goodwill, many investors will discount intangibles completely from equity.

Long-Term Investments

Long-term investments include instruments like stocks and bonds, which the company plans to hold for a period of at least one year.

Total Assets

The total value of all economic resources that a company controls, whether they are tangible or intangible, current or fixed.

Accounts Payable

Similar to accounts receivable, accounts payable is the money owed by the company that must be paid within the short term, usually one year.

Current Portion of LT Debt

The current portion of long-term debt can be thought of as a specific type of accounts payable, accounting for the money that is currently owed on long-term debt. It is usually due within one year.

Total Current Liabilities

Total current liabilities is the sum of accounts payable and the current portion of long-term debt—money that will have to be paid within the next year. In general, companies should have more current assets than current liabilities to be able to meet their financial obligations over the next year, but it is not a condition for meeting them. For example, if the value of current assets is currently insufficient, it may increase over the next several quarters through operations or long-term financing before payment is due. The difference between total current assets and total current liabilities is called "working capital," and considered a measure of liquidity—the ability to raise cash and meet short-term expenses.

Total Long-Term Debt

Long-term debt is money that is owed by the company in the longer term, typically outside of a year. In that sense, it is a noncurrent liability, which will become current over time. Healthier companies may not need to have any long-term debt on their balance sheets at all, but if they do and it is managed responsibly, the assets acquired through debt can increase a company's profitability, without needing to dilute shareholders' equity through subsequent share offerings.

Total Liabilities

The sum of all current and noncurrent liabilities owed by the company.

Common Stock

Common stock represents the sum of all money raised to date through the issuing of shares directly to investors. It can grow over time if the company issues more shares. If common stock is constantly growing, it may indicate that the company is not profitable and relies on investor cash to fund operations—a source that will inevitably dry up as shareholder value is diluted and shareholders lose interest.

In the case where the company buys back shares from investors, the value of those repurchased shares will sometimes be listed as a negative number under treasury stock (not shown in this example).

Retained Earnings

Retained earnings lists the accumulated net profit (or loss) that the company has made to date, but which has not been paid out as dividends. Every time the balance sheet is updated, retained earnings will either increase, or decrease by the net income (less dividends) reported on the income statement. This profit may be used to buy more assets or pay down debt. Some companies have negative retained earnings. This is a poor sign of a company's health, and indicates that the company has only lost money through operations to date.

Total Equity

Total equity, otherwise known as shareholders' equity, represents the portion of all assets that is owned by shareholders. This can be calculated as the difference between total assets and total liabilities (including intangibles and goodwill). Just like retained earnings, total equity can be positive or negative. If equity is negative, it means that the company may not have any liquidation value for shareholders today, and so share price is entirely speculative. This is because the amount of debt the company carries exceeds the value of their assets—a risky scenario.

Many investors calculate tangible book value as a more conservative measure in place of equity by discounting goodwill and intangibles, because they may be subject to overvaluation.

Total Common Shares Outstanding

This is the number of shares that the company has created to date. This number may grow over time should the company continue to issue shares.

You can calculate the value per share of any item on the balance sheet by dividing that item by the total common shares outstanding. For example, after calculating the tangible book value of a company, you can divide by the total common shares outstanding to arrive at the tangible book value per share. You can then compare the most recent share price on the stock market to the tangible book value per share to assess the speculative value in terms of share price—the premium or discount you are paying based on investor expectations.

It is more common to multiply the total common shares outstanding by the most recent share price to calculate the market capitalization of a company. You can then compare market capitalization to the absolute values listed on financial statements, as share price in itself is usually an incompatible measure.

The Income Statement

The income statement is used to report the profitability of a company over a given period of time. The expenses associated with revenue are broken down into various subsections, making it useful for an investor to understand where in the chain of expenses a business is most efficient or inefficient. This is typically reported each quarter, but aggregated on an annual basis as well. Profits can then be paid out as dividends, used to acquire more assets, or to pay off liabilities that appear on the balance sheet, increasing shareholders' equity. Losses will result in a loss to shareholders' equity.

It is important to understand that the income statement typically uses the accrual method of accounting. That is, the net income shown on the income statement is not necessarily the actual cash received by the company during the reporting period.[18] Instead, it represents the money *owed* to (or by) the company, which may or may not have actually been collected (or paid) over that period from operations *after* discounting noncash items like depreciation and amortization. What it does provide is a very good picture of earnings, expenses, and

---

[18] Some earnings may appear under accounts receivable, while some expenses may appear under accounts payable.

profitability. Table 2 shows the annual income statement for PRMC over several years.

Revenue

Revenue is always the top line of the balance sheet, and is the dollar amount the company receives, usually from the sale of goods or services to customers, before expenses, through regular business operations. Sometimes revenue is confused with the amount of *profit* a company makes. Profits are calculated later on the income statement, after discounting a number of different expenses. A company that demonstrates consistent or growing revenue may not be profitable.

Cost of Revenue

Cost of revenue includes the costs associated with manufacturing and delivering a product or service. Salaries are considered an indirect operational expense, and are not accounted for here.

Gross Profit

Gross profit is the difference between revenue and cost of revenue. While gross profit is a necessary condition for profitability, it is not a sufficient one. There are further expenses to be accounted for. In general, investors like to see a healthy gross profit margin, because it indicates that the company is selling a service or product for much more than the manufacturing and distribution costs.

In Millions of USD	2012	2011	2010
Revenue	1,771	1,164	925
Cost of Revenue	914	649	446
Gross Profit	857	515	479
Selling/General/Admin Expense	41	47	49
Research & Development	73	45	39
Operating Income Before Depreciation	743	423	391
Depreciation & Amortization	-160	-116	-150
Income Before Tax	583	307	241
Income Taxes	225	137	113
Net Income from Continuing Operations	358	170	128
Net Income from Discontinued Operations	360	40	-
Net Income from Total Operations	**718**	**210**	**128**
Diluted EPS	1.92	0.57	0.34
Dividends Per Share	0.23	0.08	0.06

Table 2: Annual income statement for PRMC

It is quite possible for a company to have a negative gross profit, in the case where it sells its products or services at a discount to their cost of revenue. Sometimes this is a deliberate strategy in an attempt to grow revenue and market share. However, it is unsustainable over the long term, and may be a sign of an unprofitable industry, the consequence of operational inefficiencies, or simply the result of poor management.

Selling/General/Admin Expense

Selling, General, and Administrative Expenses (SG&A) are expenses that cannot be directly linked to products or services on a per-unit basis, but which are indirectly linked to the cost of producing or delivering those services. Quite often, the bulk of this expense will be salaries and wages.

Research & Development

Activities that involve research and development are expensed here. This can be considered an investment in future growth, and may not be related directly to revenue that was realized in this quarter or year. Technology and pharmaceutical companies tend to invest more here.

Operating Income Before Depreciation

This is calculated as the difference between gross profit and the SG&A/R&D expenses. That is, this is the profit realized after discounting all direct and indirect costs from revenue.

Depreciation & Amortization

Recall that the balance sheet has a section for accumulated depreciation, which is used to recognize the decrease in value of certain tangible assets over the course of their useful life. The depreciation for this specific reporting period is accounted for here. The accumulated depreciation on the balance sheet will be updated to reflect this.

Depreciation is a noncash expense because no cash is actually spent on depreciation. The full cash amount was paid when the asset was purchased, and would have appeared one time on the cash flow statement. It is still considered an expense in the sense that it represents a very real impairment to the value of some assets.

Amortization accounts for the depreciation of intangible assets, such as patents, which have a finite lifetime before they expire and become worthless.

Income Before Tax

This represents operating income once noncash expenses have been accounted for.

Income Taxes

Income taxes must also be accounted for. Taxation rates will vary depending on where the company operates.

Net Income from Operations

This is the net income from operations after taxes.

Net Income from Discontinued Operations

While we have accounted for net income from operations, it is also important to account for income that is not related directly to operations. A good example of this is income from the sale of any assets controlled by the company. This can be a substantial amount, and so it is accounted for separately to indicate that the income derived this way may be a one-time or infrequent event, and may not reflect the operational profitability of the business.

Net Income from Total Operations

This is the sum of net income from continuing and discontinued operations. This is not necessarily the amount of cash made (or lost) by the company during the reporting period. Remember, income is usually reported on an accrual basis, and includes noncash expenses. The cash flow statement will show the *actual* cash amount made (or lost) from operations. This is a very important distinction to keep in mind, and one of the reasons why you should not overlook the cash flow statement.

Diluted EPS

Diluted EPS (earnings per share) can be calculated as the net income from total operations divided by the total number of shares that could possibly exist during the reporting period. This can be greater than the total outstanding shares found on the balance sheet (those that currently exist). Sometimes there are outstanding options for employees or investors to buy shares. These shares have not yet been created but have the potential to be in the future. Diluted in this case refers to all possible shares that could exist should all outstanding options be exercised; if all options to buy shares were exercised, the earnings relative to all outstanding shares would be diluted.

Dividends Per Share

This is the dividend (in dollars) paid out for each currently outstanding share (non-diluted). By comparing dividends per share to EPS, it is possible to have some idea about whether that dividend is safe or has the potential to grow. If the dividend per share is much less than the EPS, dividends could probably be increased should the company choose to pay out that cash rather than use it to grow by acquiring more assets or to pay down debt.

If the dividend per share is more than the EPS, the company may be paying out cash as dividends from the company's cash reserves rather than from profits generated through operations. If the company has a lot of cash, that's okay—it means that you are being "paid out" some of your equity (share price should rationally decrease to reflect this). If this occurs on a frequent basis, however, and cash is low, it may be a sign of poor management.

Some companies might issue more shares every quarter to raise the cash that is required to pay out dividends to shareholders. This might be thought of as a sort of "dividend Ponzi scheme," and something to watch out for. Many investors wonder if dividends are safe, and comparing dividends per share to EPS is one simple way of understanding that risk.

The Cash Flow Statement

Just like the income statement, the cash flow statement provides information about the company over a period of time. In this case, that information is the sources, uses, and the change in a company's cash. It is not uncommon for investors to miss the distinction between these two statements, and so they may substitute one for the other (usually looking at the income statement, but avoiding the cash flow statement).

These two statements can paint different pictures, and both should be investigated and understood. For example, where the income statement lists a noncash depreciation and amortization expense to reflect the devaluation of assets over time, the cash flow statement lists the one-time full-cash cost of an asset when it was purchased. Operational cash flow may actually be higher than net income, once noncash expenses are added back; while a company had a negative net income, it may not have lost cash—the loss might have been strictly in the devaluation of certain assets. There are fewer accounting tricks to be played here; cash is accounted for when it is spent and when it is received, and that is why some investors turn to this statement first.

There are three main sections associated with the cash flow statement: cash flow from operations, cash flow from investing activities, and cash flow from financing activities. Each section can be positive or negative, and shows the actual change in cash over the reporting period for each of these activities. The sum of these items represents the total change in cash. A more detailed analysis can be performed by breaking down each of these sections, which we will do to some extent, but the focus of this book will be on the overall importance, and high-level interpretation of these three main sections. Table 3 shows the annual cash flow statement for PRMC over several years.

Cash from Operating Activities

Whereas net income accounts for profitability using the accrual method of accounting, and includes noncash expenses, cash from operating activities reflects the actual change in cash resulting from those operations.

Cash from operating activities uses a number of items found both on the income statement and on the balance sheet, to determine the actual cash generated or lost through operations over a period of time; net income is adjusted to arrive at cash flow. In general, this involves adding back depreciation, since this is a noncash expense, plus the change in working capital (the difference between current assets and current liabilities), and the change in inventory. Net income generated through discontinued operations is subtracted under changes in other operating activities, and added to cash from discontinued operations under investing activities instead, as a matter of accounting (net income from discontinued operations is considered cash from investing activities rather than operating activities).

Note that some other items may also affect cash flow from operations, but the bottom line will give you the net flow of cash from operations (positive or negative).

In Millions of USD	2012	2011	2010
Net Income	718	210	128
Depreciation	160	116	115
Changes in Working Capital	43	51	-27
Changes in Inventory	-35	-42	1
Changes in Other Operating Activities	-360	-40	-
Cash from Operating Activities	**526**	**295**	**217**
Cash from Discontinued Operations	360	40	-
Capital Expenditures	-237	-334	-407
Cash from Investing Activities	**123**	**-294**	**-407**
Dividends Paid	-86	-30	-22
Sale of Stock	292	115	285
Increase in Debt	-	-	-
Cash from Financing Activities	**206**	**85**	**263**
Net Change in Cash	**855**	**86**	**73**
Cash at the Beginning of the Period	317	231	158
Cash at the End of the Period	1,172	317	231

Table 3: Annual cash flow statement for PRMC

Cash from Investing Activities

Cash flow from investing activities shows the change in cash resulting from the sale and purchase of longer-term assets (including financial instruments). This is where net income from discontinued operations is added back—the full amount of cash is collected on sale.

Capital expenditures (CAPEX) represent the increase in fixed assets by the company, and is a cash cost. If cash from investing activities is positive, it means that the company is primarily disposing of assets to raise cash. If cash from investing activities is negative, it means that the company is spending cash to acquire or develop long-term assets.

Cash from Financing Activities

Cash flow from financing activities represents cash paid out in the form of dividends, and/or cash raised through the sale of stock or by taking on debt. If dividends are paid, then cash is actually leaving the balance sheet. If stock is issued by the company, there will be an increase in cash. If the company borrows money, that cash will also appear on the balance sheet.

Net Change in Cash

Net change in cash represents the actual increase or decrease in cash over the reporting period as a consequence of operating, investing, and financing activities.

Investing Principles

- The balance sheet provides a snapshot of a company's financial health and value at a given moment in time; that is, its assets (the economic resources it controls), liabilities (its debts and outstanding obligations on those assets), and equity (the difference between assets and liabilities, or the portion of the assets that shareholders own).

- The income statement shows a company's profitability over a period of time, including revenue, expenses, and net income. The income statement also recognizes noncash expenses like depreciation and amortization. Income is reported on an accrual basis, meaning that while those sales and expenses have been recorded over the period, the cash made (or lost) may not have been collected (or spent) yet.

- The cash flow statement shows the sources and uses of cash over a period of time from operational, investing, and financing activities. This statement is frequently overlooked by investors.

4
Measures of Valuation

One of the ways to evaluate and compare a company's financial information is to use financial ratios. There are many common ratios that can be used to establish value, profitability, and liquidity. These ratios can be evaluated in absolute terms or in relative terms to peer companies to determine which one might be a better investment. It is not uncommon for some of these ratios to be pre-calculated for you based on the previous year's financial results, or on projected performance, and presented near share price on investing websites. Of course, a ratio in itself doesn't paint the entire picture, and so understanding these ratios—their limitations and assumptions—is critical.

It is important to realize that many of these ratios rely on previous financial data. In some industries, this can be a meaningful predictor of future performance, while in others a more forward-looking understanding of a company's operations is required.

Profitability

Price to Earnings (P/E)

The P/E ratio is one of the most commonly used ratios. This is probably because it is one of the simplest ratios to understand. While it is a useful measure, it is important to understand that it has limitations. A good P/E is not a sufficient condition for a good investment; one must consider other metrics as well.

P/E is most commonly calculated as the ratio between share price and the previous year's EPS (sometimes called the trailing P/E). However, it is sometimes useful to calculate a forward P/E based on projected future earnings (these projections usually come from analysts), provided that future earnings can be reasonably estimated. It can also be calculated as the ratio of market capitalization to net income.

$$P/E = \frac{\text{Stock Price}}{\text{Earnings Per Share (EPS)}}$$

Sometimes the P/E can be very low (less than five), and sometimes it can be a multiple of hundreds or even thousands—a special growth case where investors expect earnings to grow significantly in the future, dropping the ratio over time (sometimes investors are wrong).

Note that EPS can include single-time occurrences like the sale of a fixed asset. In such a case, P/E may be lower than one would otherwise calculate from continuing operations alone. For this reason, it is very important to understand where the EPS is coming from.

P/E says nothing about a company's liquidity, or the current tangible book value per share. It is an earnings ratio and nothing more, but it can be very useful when compared between different companies. For example, all else held equal, you might be better off investing in the company that has the lower P/E.

Gross Profit Margin

The gross profit margin represents the level of profit (or loss) a company makes from revenue when accounting only for the direct costs associated with the production and distribution of products and services. Gross profit margins can vary quite a lot depending on the company and industry. Some retail businesses can have very small gross profit margins, whereas companies that deliver software or services can have very high gross profit margins. If the gross profit margin is negative (meaning that gross profit is also negative), then the company is losing money even before accounting for SG&A expenses.

$$\text{Gross Profit Margin} = \frac{\text{Gross Profit}}{\text{Revenue}}$$

Remember, while a positive gross profit margin is a necessary condition for profitability, it is not, in itself, a sufficient one. If a company has an excellent gross profit margin, but very high SG&A expenses, it may still be losing money. In general, a higher gross profit margin is more desirable.

Net Profit Margin

Whereas gross profit margin accounts only for the cost of revenue that is directly associated with manufacturing and delivering a product or service, net profit margin accounts for *all* indirect expenses as well. Just like the gross profit margin, the net profit margin can vary considerably between businesses and industries. Profitable businesses must have a positive net profit margin. Larger net profit margins are better.

$$\text{Net Profit Margin} = \frac{\text{Net Income}}{\text{Revenue}}$$

Return on Assets (ROA)

Return on assets is a measure of how profitable a company is in relation to the assets that it controls. ROA is calculated as the ratio of net income to total assets controlled by the company.

$$\text{ROA} = \frac{\text{Net Income}}{\text{Total Assets}}$$

This gives you some idea of how efficiently a company makes use of the assets that it controls to generate income.

While higher ratios are better, ROA is best used when compared between companies in the same industry.

Return on Equity (ROE)

Return on equity is a measure of how profitable a company is in relation to the amount of equity owned by shareholders. ROE is calculated as the ratio of net income to total equity. This gives you some idea of how efficiently a company makes use of the equity that shareholders own to generate income.

$$ROE = \frac{\text{Net Income}}{\text{Total Equity}}$$

Value

Price to Book (P/B)

Whereas P/E is a ratio that compares share price to earnings, P/B is a measure of share price relative to tangible book value. This is probably the most important ratio used by value investors (those looking to pay less than the estimated liquidation value of a company). P/B is calculated as the ratio of market capitalization to tangible book value (equity less goodwill and intangibles).[19]

If the P/B is less than one, you are paying less than the present tangible book value of the company per share. It is

---

[19] Although sometimes it uses equity in place of tangible book value.

generally rare to find companies that are valued this way by the market. There are two possible reasons for a company to have a low P/B. First, it is possible that the market has severely undervalued the company, and indeed this is sometimes the case. Investors should be cautious, however, that sometimes companies are awarded a low P/B because the company is losing (or expected to lose) money, and the future tangible book value per share could be quite less (or worse, zero, in the case of bankruptcy). So, just like P/E, you cannot make a sound investment decision based on P/B alone.

Buying shares in a company with a very high P/B means that you are paying a substantial speculative premium on your shares. The current liquidation value is quite small. All else held equal, an investor should like to invest in companies with a lower P/B ratio.

$$P/B = \frac{\text{Market Capitalization}}{\text{Total Equity} - (\text{Goodwill} + \text{Intangibles})}$$

Dividend Yield

Dividend yield is the ratio of the annual dividends paid out by the company per share divided by the current price per share. It is commonly expressed as a percentage.

$$\text{Dividend Yield} = \frac{\text{Annual Dividends Per Share}}{\text{Price Per Share}}$$

Higher dividends are great, provided the company is generating them through operations, and not simply paying them out from their existing cash reserves while experiencing operational losses.

Dividend Payout Ratio

The dividend payout ratio is the ratio of total dividends to net income over a reporting period. If the dividend payout ratio is exactly one, then the company is paying out all net income to investors, rather than growing the company. If the dividend payout ratio is greater than one, then the company is paying out a higher dividend than it is making from operations—the company is effectively returning existing shareholders' equity to investors. This is unsustainable over the long term.

$$\text{Dividend Payout Ratio} = \frac{\text{Total Dividends}}{\text{Net Income}}$$

Net Present Value

Net present value (NPV) is defined to be the net difference between the present value[20] of all future cash inflows and outflows, including earnings, operational

---

[20] The present value of cash is related to an important principle known as the "time value of money." In general, this means that $100 invested today is worth more than $100 in the future, because of interest over time. Or, a series of cash flows over time can be calculated to be equal to an equivalent lump sum today, where each future payment is discounted by the interest rate.

expenditures, and capital expenditures over the life of a project. It estimates a number to answer the question, "What is this project worth today?" If the NPV is negative, it means that the project or development would likely be unprofitable; cash outflows would exceed cash inflows over the course of the project. These calculations are done internally, and sometimes presented to investors as a means to value large or complex projects.

This book does not focus on the calculation of NPV. In most relevant cases the company will calculate it and present it to you. However, it is important for an investor to understand what it means, and to recognize if the company has made it clear what the NPV is for a large capital project (has it done a clear and transparent analysis?). Of course, NPV is subject to a number of variables. For this reason, it is not unusual to see a number of different NPVs calculated under different scenarios.

NPVs are often calculated at different discount rates, expressed as percentages, which can be used as a means of accounting for possible risk, and financing costs associated large capital expenditures. Along with various discount rates, you may see Internal Rates of Return (IRR), which represent the effective interest rate(s) of the project. Generally speaking, a project with a higher NPV and a higher IRR is expected to be more rewarding. NPV can be calculated through discounted cash flow (DCF) analysis. If you are investing in resource companies, you are encouraged to learn more about this.

Resource Properties

Resource properties have value because of the finite resource(s) they contain. These properties require additional consideration when it comes to appropriate valuation, which goes beyond the balance sheet.

For example, sometimes land is acquired for exploration by a mining company. The price paid for that land is recorded on the balance sheet. Remember, property never appreciates on the balance sheet, even if it would be worth more in a sale. This is a conservative method of accounting, and is the standard that is often followed[21]. If, however, the company makes a discovery, or finds higher levels of resources on that property than previously indicated, this information is not always reflected in the financial value of the property that is listed on the balance sheet.

How can you estimate the value of a resource property? There may be quite a few variables to consider, including resource grades (g/ton), indicated reserves, operational lifetime, and the cost of extraction. This type of analysis is not straightforward. It's messy and it takes some experience to really understand it; and even if you do understand it, you will realize that it depends on a lot of assumptions. For this reason, a NPV will usually be estimated for you by serious companies. If a mining company has not established an NPV for its mine, an investor should recognize this.

Just because the NPV is positive and attractive, does not necessarily mean that the company will be able to develop the

---

[21] This is always the case under GAAP. IFRS has some flexibility here, under certain circumstances. As mentioned in Chapter 3, this book follows the GAAP convention for asset valuation because it is both more conservative and commonly used in the United States.

property. Capital expenditures can be very high (in the hundreds of millions of dollars or more), and so the company that explores the property may be unable to develop it without securing funding, through a loan, equity offerings, or development agreements with other companies.

The NPV may also be overestimated—costs often run higher than expected. These projects can be very complex, carrying a number of risks over a long period of time.

Liquidity

Current Ratio

The current ratio is calculated as the ratio of current assets to current liabilities (assets that should be capable of being converted to cash in a period of less than a year, and outstanding debts that are owed within that same period).

$$\text{Current Ratio} = \frac{\text{Current Assets}}{\text{Current Liabilities}}$$

This is a measure of short-term liquidity. That is, the company's ability to pay its short-term debt obligations. Having a current ratio of less than one is never a good sign. However, it does not always indicate bankruptcy, as there may be ways to increase current assets through long-term financing, share offerings, or even operations before current liabilities are due. Generally speaking, having a current ratio of two or greater is a sign of a healthier company.

Working Capital

Working capital, like the current ratio, is a measure of liquidity. However, it is calculated as the difference between current assets and current liabilities, rather than as a ratio.[22] In general, both measures can be interpreted in the same way, and provide roughly the same information. Both are commonly used, and so both have been included (working capital is an item on the cash flow statement). A negative working capital should be considered to be as bad as a current ratio of less than one.

$$\text{Working Capital} = \text{Current Assets} - \text{Current Liabilities}$$

Debt

Debt to Equity

The debt-to-equity ratio is a measure of the portion of assets that is funded through debt (liabilities) to the portion of assets that is fully owned by shareholders (equity).

$$\text{Debt to Equity} = \frac{\text{Total Liabilities}}{\text{Total Equity}}$$

---

[22] When it comes to investing, meaningful calculations need not be complex.

A high debt-to-equity ratio indicates that the company is highly leveraged, meaning that it controls a lot of assets that are funded through outstanding debt. If done carefully, this allows a business to make use of a greater number of assets to increase its earning power, but not without risk.

Cash Flow

Operating Cash Flow/Sales Ratio

The operating cash flow/sales ratio is similar to the net profit margin ratio, except that it measures the actual cash generated on sales during the reporting period relative to revenue, and not just the income that was recorded. A higher operational cash flow to sales ratio is better.

$$\text{Operating Cash Flow/ Sales Ratio} = \frac{\text{Operating Cash Flow}}{\text{Revenue}}$$

Free Cash Flow (FCF)

Free cash flow represents the cash a company is able to generate from operations during a reporting period after capital expenditures are accounted for (money used to expand and/or develop the company's assets). This is calculated by subtracting capital expenditures from cash generated from operating activities. Generally speaking, investors like to see a nice positive FCF, but a negative FCF is not necessarily a bad thing; it may mean that the company is strategically reinvesting its cash from operations to expand its assets base.

FCF = Cash From Operations − Capital Expenditures

Investing Principles

- Financial ratios are a common way of summarizing and interpreting financial information, allowing an investor to make meaningful comparisons between companies.

- It is important to use multiple ratios, focusing on areas like profitability, valuation, liquidity, debt, and cash flow.

- Ratios can be skewed by one-time occurrences, and so an investor must be diligent to understand the underlying variables.

- NPV is useful to estimate the feasibility and value of complex projects.

- It is impossible to value a resource company based on financial statements alone. Property assets are frequently listed at their purchase price, even if they are worth more through subsequent exploration and property assessment. If you are going to invest in resource companies, you must employ a more rigorous investigation of the company's underlying assets, and a forward-looking assessment of their future operational costs and cash flow.

- Never rely strictly on financial ratios. It is important to examine a company's financial statements directly as well.

5

Investment Decision Making

So, how do you actually make investment decisions? While the previous chapters have focused on specific elements of investing, including how to read financial statements, and basic valuation techniques, this chapter tries to bring the broader picture into focus.

Every investment you make is an important decision. This decision can be made most effectively by understanding just what it is you are buying—by analyzing the financial information and documentation that the company makes public. It is important to recognize not only value, but also the potential risk that you might face when investing in a company. For example, a company with an attractive price-to-book ratio today might also be unprofitable, and so that value might disappear over time. You can then attempt to minimize this risk by being selective with your investments. Try to seek out the opportunities that would best warrant your capital, by purchasing quality businesses that have been underpriced by the market.

First, it is important to understand that a higher risk does not necessarily mean a higher possible reward. Certainly, in some cases this can be true, but it is not something that you should ever assume. Some very risky companies can be priced at substantial premiums, leaving little in the way of reward should they succeed. At the same time, some great companies with solid financials and excellent growth prospects can be substantially undervalued by the market. Only through a careful and rational assessment, including the use of some of the analysis tools outlined in the previous chapters, can you begin to make these distinctions. Otherwise, you really are just gambling.

Speculating or Investing

It is useful to separate the process of "buying stocks" into two very separate categories. These two classifications— "investing" and "speculating"—were famously described by Benjamin Graham in his book *The Intelligent Investor*.[23]

In this framework, investing assumes that you are actually evaluating a company using financial information, assessing risk, and purchasing shares with the intent to hold them for a longer period of time unless a good opportunity arises to sell. You are not investing simply by buying shares in a company that is large, has a popular product, and a strong brand; these are not sufficient conditions. The company must have solid fundamentals (income, cash flow, and equity) at an

---

[23] *The Intelligent Investor*, first published in 1949, contains a number of valuable insights when it comes to investing, and remains quite relevant even today.

attractive price—an appropriate speculative premium, or even discount to tangible book value.

Speculating, on the other hand, typically means that you are buying shares in a company with more of a hope for positive returns in the future. There are two types of speculation.

The first type of speculation occurs when you are knowingly aware of the risks. For example, you might invest in a company that is losing money, but you are aware of that fact, and expect it to change in the future. This form of speculation is okay provided you understand the risks and you are prepared to lose your investment. You never want to allocate too much money to knowingly speculative investments, though in such cases, the rewards might actually be much higher.

The second form of speculation occurs when you are not aware of the risks—when you purchase shares with the hope that you can sell them later at a higher price. This should be avoided at all costs. You might be buying shares in a company that is about to file for bankruptcy.

In general, speculating usually involves taking on a much higher degree of risk, and should never be confused with the discipline required of investing and financial analysis.

Identifying Stocks

So, where do you start when you want to identify a stock to invest in? There are two general approaches: the top-down approach and the bottom-up approach.

When it comes to the top-down approach, the news and media can be a good place to start. In this case, you may hear about a sector or company, and then do your own research to investigate the company and its current valuation relative to other industries and its peers.

In the bottom-up approach, you begin with a set of quantitative investment criteria like P/E, P/B, market capitalization, and net profit margin (the criteria and thresholds you use are up to you), and screen for companies that meet these criteria. To achieve this, an investor can make use of a stock screener. This is a tool provided by many financial websites, allowing you to quickly sift through all of the companies on a given exchange.

Both of these approaches allow you to *identify* potential investments, but this is only where your analysis should begin.

News and Media

Stocks are a hot topic for many news and media outlets. There are a number of publications and news networks that focus exclusively on the stock market. This can be both good and bad. First, the bad: for just about every large, publicly traded company you can think of, there will be a number of analysts who cover it. Their opinions will often vary, and they will frequently reassess their price targets in response to the market (reacting rather than forecasting), or be flat-out incorrect in their assessments. For this reason, it is very important to do your own research. Never rely on subjective assessments or vague statements like, "We see this as a good investment, and we see this going well beyond where it is currently." It's easy for investors to have a false sense of confidence about such statements, especially if they reinforce their own beliefs.

However, there are two clear advantages to financial news and media. First, they can keep you in check. You may hear an opinion based on real figures and numbers that are worth considering. This might conflict with what you had originally believed. This doesn't necessarily mean that you should panic, but it does provide a check for your own investment thesis. Secondly, there may very well be good companies mentioned that do warrant your attention.

Therefore, the subjective coverage and ratings of the news and media should never be taken for granted, or dismissed, but rather used to provide checks and balances on your own analysis.

Finally, it is not unusual for the CEOs of many large companies to participate in interviews on major investment networks. These interviews can provide clear insight into the vision senior management has for the company.

Stock Screeners

Stock screeners allow you to screen for companies based on quantitative financial variables. You can screen based on just about anything, from the company's size and industry to the financial ratios described earlier. Most banks and brokerage firms will provide these stock screeners, but so will many investment news sites. Find one that you are comfortable with.

After identifying these companies, you must then do a thorough analysis of their financial information to look for anything that is out of place. For example, a company's P/E ratio may be inflated due to earnings from discontinued operations, and so may not be representative of what its P/E will be next year.

There may also be certain events that could influence future earnings, so ratios based on previous financial data are not necessarily an indication of what investors can expect in the future. For example, a mining company might be expecting a significant increase in operational costs, which is not reflected in currently reported financial ratios.

A stock screener can also miss companies that have tremendous investment potential while presently demonstrating no earnings.

Evaluating a Business

What's a share *really* worth? Many people will tell you that it's worth the share price, because that's what the market is willing to pay. This isn't always true. The market makes mistakes all the time.

Assuming that the current share price accurately reflects the underlying share value is one of the most innocent mistakes an investor can make, and undoubtedly the greatest risk most undertake. Price is often a lousy indicator of value. Before a company goes bankrupt, you can be sure somebody somewhere purchased some of its shares for something, because they didn't understand the risks. He or she will probably tell you it wasn't worth the price they paid.

While this book attempts to make the big picture clearer, and present a meaningful interpretation of many of the individual components to making investment decisions, it is incomplete. Ultimately, readers will have to, through their own reflection, piece everything together and weigh the variables under circumstances that are subject to change. This is only a starting point. Keep this in mind. One of the ways to do this is to practice analyzing different companies.

The only way to even begin performing any sort of valuation is to *actually* look at a company's financial information. Valuation has a strict quantitative requirement — what are the numbers? This is something that many investors and traders will avoid altogether, and it couldn't be riskier. Step through a company's income statement, balance sheet, and cash flow statement, and compare them to those of peer companies to get a sense of how this company is performing both on an absolute and on a relative basis. In the case of resource stocks, one must go a step further to understand the value of the company's property assets — what is the NPV of its project(s)?

Of course, the decision to invest in something should depend not only on the financial health and profitability of a business, but also on the premium or discount that you pay. It helps to understand what the speculative value is. You can estimate this quite easily — just subtract tangible book value from market capitalization. The more conventional way to do this is to calculate the P/B ratio. Determining if it is in your interest is the bigger question. Just because you're in something with a smaller speculative premium doesn't rule out risk completely.

Do you think the market is underestimating or overestimating the future value of the company? Markets are made up of people, and people make mistakes. Large sums of money flow in and out of stocks for a variety of reasons that can significantly influence share price. Low-volume stocks can experience drastic swings through the buying and selling of only a few investors, be it rational or not.

Remember, risk and value are two sides to the same coin. In order to assess value, you must have some understanding of the risk. Don't expect anybody to do this for you. Many companies declare bankruptcy with little warning. Those investors who do their due diligence won't need anybody to tell them that a company is at risk of bankruptcy.

Analyzing the Balance Sheet

A good place to start is with the balance sheet. What's the equity? Is it positive or negative? What if you discount goodwill and intangibles; is tangible book value still positive? If equity (or, more conservatively, tangible book value) is *negative*, this is an entirely speculative investment. The current liquidation value for investors is then probably zero. If you are investing in a company with negative equity, you should confirm that there is a feasible plan for the company going forward. If there is no plan, you probably shouldn't be investing in this company.

If tangible book value is positive, is it much greater or much less than the current market capitalization (what's the speculative value)? In general, all else held equal, one would prefer to buy stocks that have a lower P/B ratio. Of course, that is not a sufficient condition for a good investment. If the P/B ratio is less than one, it means that speculative value is negative—the market thinks this company is going to *lose* money in the future. Maybe the market is right; you have to look at the nature of the business's operations. If the market is wrong, this could be a great stock to invest in.

Equity is composed of two parts: common stock (the amount of money raised through stock offerings to the public), and retained earnings (the accumulated net income that has not been paid out as dividends, generated through operations). Equity might be positive only because of capital raised through common stock. Retained earnings could be negative, having eaten away at that equity—in this case there has been no return on the initial common stock investment. Therefore, negative retained earnings are a red flag. One would prefer to see positive retained earnings—an indication that the company has accumulated net income, thereby increasing shareholder's equity through *operations*. Therefore, it is very important to look at what makes up equity, and not simply take the number for granted.

At this point, one should have some idea of what the equity is (the value that belongs to shareholders, today) and its composition. This can then be compared to the current market capitalization. This allows one to determine the premium, or discount today between what investors *pay* and what shareholders *own* (whether such a premium or discount is warranted is a matter of further investigation). How much are you paying, for how much equity?

Next, one should look at the liabilities section. Does the company have any debt? If not, that's great. If so, is it a lot relative to equity? Is there a good reason for that debt? For example, that debt may have been raised to finance a large capital expenditure to avoid diluting shareholder value. Did the company put together a solid feasibility study justifying that loan? In other words, is that debt the result of good business decision making, or just a financial risk?

In general, one would prefer to invest in a company that has zero debt; one that can finance everything on its own.

Companies with a lot of debt are said to be heavily leveraged. That means that they have accumulated most or even all of their assets through debt, so while they control them, shareholders don't actually own them. Some industries, such as banking and financial services, rely heavily on debt, but if a company has a significant amount of debt relative to its peers and little to show for it, it may be a sign of poor management.

Current liabilities are owed within the next year. Does the company have enough current assets to cover those liabilities? If it doesn't, can you be sure that it will be able to generate enough cash through operations, financing, or further equity dilution in time?

Finally, it is a good exercise to look at the company's assets. Are they heavy on cash, unsold inventory, property, or equipment?

Now that you understand the premium (or discount) you are paying, and the underlying company's financial health, you can try to understand how the company makes (or loses) money in an attempt to determine what the value of the company might be in the future (is that premium or discount *attractive*).

Analyzing the Income Statement

The income statement is best analyzed in sequence starting at the top. First, is there revenue? If there isn't, you have to ask yourself why. What's the gross profit? Is it positive or negative?

Companies need to make money to provide a return to shareholders. If a company has a negative gross profit, it means that its cost of revenue (costs directly associated with materials, manufacturing, and delivery of goods or services sold, excluding salaries and indirect expenses) exceeds its revenue for that period. This might be a strategic move in order to try and gain market share, but frequently it's a sign of poor management, or a bad industry to be in. Investors should seek out companies with positive (and hopefully good-sized) gross margins. Remember that even after gross profit, there are usually going to be further SG&A and possibly R&D expenses. A company with a consistently negative gross profit should be examined carefully—if these losses are happening under normal business operations, it might be a bad sign. If the stock is trading at a speculative premium, it may be a better idea to look elsewhere.

Take a look at the company's SG&A and R&D expenses. Are they fairly constant, or are they increasing? Do they increase when revenues increase? If so, it may be that employees are given extra compensation for the company's performance. While this might be great for them, that extra compensation may reduce the EPS that shareholders see. That is, even though a company had an excellent quarter, investors may not be the ones to see the rewards.

What's the net income? If a company has a negative net income, it means that its operations as a whole are losing money. That's not good, and it's unsustainable over the long term. Is this a trend? Is there any reason to expect it to change (perhaps a mining company hasn't entered production yet)? Remember that one-time, unusual expenses can affect net income. If they made money by selling large assets, you should note that as an unusual occurrence, because it might have resulted in a higher net income than usual.

If you are invested in a business that is losing money, it is important to keep a close eye on its cash balance and current (liquid) assets relative to current liabilities. If the company is running out of cash, it will probably need to raise capital (if it is possible) or it may face bankruptcy.

Finally, some companies pay out dividends to shareholders. This might be small or large, depending on the nature of the business. Many people look at increasing dividends over time as a positive thing, but one needs to be sure of where those dividends are coming from. If you're wondering whether a dividend is safe, the answer is that you can never really know—that's a decision for the company's management. You can, however, determine if that dividend is being paid out from profits or from the company's cash reserves. If the dividend per share exceeds the EPS, all the company is doing is returning some of your equity to you, at the expense of the company's cash reserves—cash that the company may need, especially if they are currently unprofitable. To provide value, dividends need to come from *operations*. Sometimes a company will pay out the usual dividend, even if it exceeds its EPS for that quarter, if it's an unusual occurrence for earnings to be so low, because shareholders have come to expect a specific dividend.

Analyzing the Cash Flow Statement

Having investigated the company's current financial health and value from the balance sheet relative to market capitalization (the premium or discount investors pay today), and profitability from the income statement, it is important to examine its cash flows. Cash is important—where's it coming from, or going to?

Many investors ignore the cash flow statement altogether because they believe that the income statement already reflects that information. It does not. Remember, the income statement includes noncash expenses, like depreciation, and represents invoiced sales and expenses on an accrual basis; this is not necessarily the cash that has actually been spent or received in that period. Some investors like to look at the cash flow statement *first*. This gives them a clear breakdown of whether cash is being made or lost through operations. It also includes the change in the company's cash once all sources and uses of cash for investing and financing have been accounted for.

One might begin by comparing net income with the cash flow from operations. These values ought to be similar. If anything, cash flow from operations might actually be higher once you add back depreciation (which doesn't actually affect a company's cash—that cash was spent when the asset was acquired). If net income is positive, so should be the cash flow from operations. Otherwise, it is worth investigating what's going on. If the company is slow to collect cash from sales (a growing accounts receivable), is there a risk that that cash is never collected because a customer declares bankruptcy? If operational cash flow is unexpectedly high, is it simply because of a short term change in working capital, where the company has a growing accounts payable (money they owe that they haven't paid yet)?

Having examined cash flow from operations, we can then examine the sources and uses of cash from investing and financing activities. Was cash raised through an equity offering or a loan? Were there any significant capital expenditures, where cash was spent to acquire or develop an important asset?

At this point, you should have some sense of the company's financial situation—the value you get *today* for the price you pay for shares, and the company's profitability and cash flow, which help you to understand how that value might change in the *future*.

This has been a high level overview of the items you might want to look at. Ultimately, you will need to quantify these variables, compare them to other companies, and try to understand what might happen going forwards.

Company Information

Most publicly listed companies will have a website with information for investors. You should familiarize yourself with this information. Corporate presentations are of particular interest—these presentations often provide useful summaries of important information that may not be clearly listed elsewhere. For example, mining companies may compare their expected capital expenditures and operating costs in absolute and relative amounts to those of their peers. They may also discuss proven and probable resources, drilling information, the grade of material, and even the methods of extraction and processing. A lot of this information might otherwise be buried in lengthy technical reports.

Resource companies beyond the exploration stage[24] should provide clear feasibility studies and estimated cash flows. These reports should be detailed, and the company should provide a clear high-level summary and NPV for each of its assets.

Weigh the Competition

Investing is all about allocating your capital in the best possible way. Therefore, a "good" investment is defined not

---

[24] The exploration stage is inherently speculative.

only in absolute terms but also in relative terms. There may be several "good" investments (there might be none). You want to try to find the best one(s). Never limit your analysis to a single company; test that valuation against its competitors—is there better value? Of course, you shouldn't limit yourself to a single sector either. It may very well be that the "best" investment in a sector is lousy compared to other opportunities in other sectors.

Tracking Investments

Price and News Alerts

Besides their quarterly financial announcements, many companies will issue press releases, often without any warning, on material transactions, including acquisition or funding updates, contracts, and sales information. This information can have a significant impact on share value, and therefore on share price, by adjusting the conditions of risk and value relative to the previous market valuation. It may have no impact if this information was already assumed or "priced in."

Through your investment account, or other investing news services, you can often subscribe (for free) to news releases from companies that you select, e-mailed to you shortly after they are made available. For companies whose operations are heavily tied to such information, it is recommended that you subscribe to these alerts.

Google Alerts provides an easy way to receive e-mail alerts on keywords that appear in the news, and can also be quite useful. You can enter alerts for company names, products, or industries to receive any Google News updates.

In terms of price, the *last* stock price, and current bid/ask prices and volumes are sometimes called Level 1 price information. This information is public and easily accessible.[25] Of course, it is important to understand that below the current bid price and above the current ask price there are additional buy and sell orders of different volumes that investors have placed, referred to as the "market depth." This information, called Level 2 data, is typically provided to investors by exchanges for a monthly fee.

In general, a long-term investor should not need to be too concerned about market depth. If you understand the current value, you can decide whether the current market price being offered by some investors represents a good investment opportunity or not—you don't get to choose the price investors are willing to sell for. However, it is useful to be aware that such information is available. For some investors, it can be a helpful exercise to examine the Level 2 data to understand the concept of market depth, and to appreciate that current share price only reflects a limited number of transactions. For this reason, you might consider subscribing for, say, a limited period of time for educational purposes.

Of course, the market depth is never static, and should not be relied upon. It has been reported that some larger traders and/or trading algorithms sometimes generate brief buy or sell orders above or below the current price and quickly remove them, as part of their trading strategy.

---

[25] Sometimes this information is delayed by fifteen minutes or so, unless you subscribe directly to the exchange.

Insider Activity

Insiders, including high-level executives and members of the board of directors of public companies, are required to report all transactions related to their buying and selling of shares in that company. This information can be both useful and misleading.[26] If executives are selling substantial portions of their shares, it may be a sign that they are bailing out. At the same time, if they were to buy many shares on the open market, it may mean that they are very confident in the future of the company and the price they are paying today for the value they might get in the future (that doesn't necessarily make them *right*).

In an effort to avoid misleading investors, many companies have adopted automatic disposition plans to allow executives to sell the options they are granted as a means of compensation. This means that on specific dates they will automatically sell some of their shares, whatever the price happens to be.

Note that if the insider activity lists that shares were purchased on the open market, it usually means that the insider purchased shares with their own money.

Selling

Knowing when to sell can be just as, if not more difficult than, the decision to buy. Do you take the profit, take the loss, or do nothing? There is no obvious rule for selling; however, if we were to follow the definition for investing that was introduced earlier, we might say selling is the process of

---

[26] Sometimes insiders report their activity incorrectly. This might include reporting that they have purchased shares, when in fact they have sold them.

identifying those companies that you own whose speculative value has been overestimated by the market, or equivalently, when the market capitalization represents an unrealistically high valuation for the business.

If your investments are down in price, should you sell? The answer is that it depends. Have the fundamentals changed? Has there been a material change in the company's prospects going forward? Did the company underestimate costs? Is there new competition, which did not exist when you purchased stock that could affect its revenue? Is the projected valuation going to be lower in the future?

If there is no obvious change in fundamentals, you may not want to sell. However, if there has been, and certainly if there is a short-term risk of bankruptcy, you should carefully consider selling and taking the loss.

When your investments are up, you might ask yourself a similar question—is the business worth the current market capitalization? Will the company ever be worth it? If you think it might be, you may want to hold. If you think it's overvalued, you should probably sell. Others will take a simpler approach. If they are up by a certain amount, they may sell regardless of the fundamentals. This is a matter of preference for the individual investor—it's a free market.

When selling, it is important to consider the fundamentals and perform the same risk and valuation analysis as when you are buying. The difference is that your analysis is limited to the stocks that you currently hold. You need to consider the value going forwards and act accordingly. Sometimes it's time to take the profit—or loss. Not every business succeeds.

Buying Opportunities

What does it mean to buy low? Does it mean buying low on the day, on the month, or on the year? In terms of price, it can mean any of these things. But to investors, buying low should mean more than just price. It should mean buying at a discount—buying for less than the tangible book value, or when the speculative value is being severely underestimated by the market. If you can buy shares in a stable and profitable company for less than its tangible book value, you may have found a bargain. Unfortunately, it can be difficult to find these companies. You can screen for them, but they may not exist when you do.

Emotion plays a big part in the stock market. Historically speaking, periods after the stock market has crashed have presented enormous buying opportunities, while at the same time presenting enormous risk. To differentiate, you have to look at individual companies—not just price.

Many large funds may sell significant portions of their portfolio without considering whether it makes sense to sell or not—they may have no choice. Stop-limit orders may be triggered. Many traders who follow price movements alone will read "bearish[27] technicals"—what just about anybody would recognize as a downward movement in share price—and sell, whether it makes sense or not. For the investor who understands value, liquidity, and basic financial analysis, this is where you will find the bargains.

---

[27] "Bullish" and "bearish" refer to upward and downward market trends, respectively. People who expect the market to go up or down are sometimes called "bulls" or "bears."

If you are fortunate enough to have the cash, careful, and are prepared to invest, stock market crashes can present enormous opportunities. At the same time, bad companies will also trade at low prices, and there may not be such a thing as a bargain for a company that has no earnings, no equity, and is at risk of bankruptcy.

Diversification

In the world of investing, diversification has become cliché, but that doesn't make it any less important. If you are planning on investing a significant amount of your savings and capital, you must diversify. Some people look at this as a way of spreading your bets, when you don't know for certain which one will be "the winner."

However, sometimes it's better to take a more conservative view. Diversification is important because every investor makes mistakes, and making one of those mistakes with most or all of your savings is not a situation you want to be in. Without question, *many* investors have found themselves in this position. There is a tendency to assume that most investors are making money, but this simply isn't always the case. Many businesses that are listed on exchanges are highly unprofitable, and will inevitably go out of business. People invest in these businesses. You will see daily trading volume. For every seller there must be a buyer.

There is no hard-and-fast rule for diversifying, but in general it means diversification not only between companies, but between industries as well. This doesn't mean that you should buy stocks in every sector. Some sectors may be much less profitable and/or riskier than others. This is where some research and thought is important.

Mutual funds and exchange-traded funds (ETFs) can be an excellent way of giving you diversified exposure, depending on the fund(s) you choose to invest in. For many investors, this means peace of mind. *Even* if the stock market crashes, your exposure may be no worse off than that of many other investors, and so you are effectively "in the same boat," and not in the water.

While one should always seek to diversify, diversification in itself is no guarantee. One should always understand and profile the underlying investments for risk and value.

Investing Principles

- Every investment opportunity is unique, and requires different risks to be weighed under circumstances that are subject to change.

- Stock screeners allow you to filter companies based on objective criteria. Even then, always check out their financial information.

- Calculate the speculative premium (or discount) and ask yourself if you're getting a good deal. What's the value? Are there risks on the company's balance sheet? Are they profitable? How might shareholders' equity change in the future? Is it the best allocation of capital you can make?

- Insider buying and selling activity can be a useful indicator, but it can also be misleading, depending on whether the company has adopted an automatic disposition plan or not.

- Price and news alerts can be very useful if you are invested in volatile companies or industries.

- The best buying opportunities frequently present themselves when the market is most fearful, but always be wary of what you are buying.

- Diversification is important because everybody makes mistakes.

6

Risk Factors

This chapter covers a number of different types of risks that an investor might encounter, beyond the scope of what has been covered so far. Up until this point, the assessment of risk has largely been limited to information that is available on a company's financial statements.

This survey of risk is by no means exhaustive, but rather it is intended to broaden your understanding of the full range of what is possible. As an investor, you must recognize that it is important to develop your understanding of all types of risk that can exist—those that are directly financial *and* those that are not. Understand that some of these risks cannot be controlled for. For example, investors put their trust in those who control a company on their behalf, but sometimes that trust is broken—serious cases of financial fraud have occurred that have cost investors enormous amounts of money.

If you are investing your own money directly, you can't expect anybody to assess the risks for you.

Financial Risks

Financing Risks

Sometimes a company will need to spend a significant amount of capital to acquire, or to develop an asset. This asset could be a mine or an expensive industrial process. Capital expenditures can amount to hundreds of millions of dollars, or more—money that the company may not have. For this reason, investors should be conscious of the business's ability to raise that money, if it does not already have it in the first place. The company may need to raise that money by issuing more shares or by taking on debt.

However, if market conditions are poor, it may be unable to issue shares. If the company needs to raise money through a debt placement, lenders may refuse. This can have a significant impact on a company's ability to do business. For this reason, investors need to be aware of a business's ability to finance or raise capital for any large, outstanding capital expenditures.

Cost Overruns

Sometimes a company's actual expenses exceed its original estimates. When a company encounters expenses well in excess of what it had planned or even budgeted for, we call it a cost overrun. It is important for an investor to weigh carefully the projected expenses reported by a company. For example, other companies might have similar projects where you can use their costs as a reference. If the company projects a range of possible expenses, it's usually a good idea to use its most conservative estimate. Otherwise, consider adding some margin of safety to those expenses in your analysis. If the success of the business hinges on a small margin, then one should be aware of this.

Unusual Expenses

Some expenses appear one time, and are not a part of normal operations. These expenses are usually unexpected. While unusual expenses might not recur, they can have a significant impact on a business's earnings, or even value. Some unusual expenses can mean the difference between a healthy, profitable quarter and a substantial loss to shareholders' equity.

Impaired Assets

Sometimes the value of an asset listed on a company's balance sheet is worth much less than what was originally reported. Goodwill is a common example of an intangible asset that can become impaired. If the premium paid for an acquisition proves to be worth less than originally accounted for under goodwill (e.g., software or technology that is purchased becomes obsolete or uncompetitive), it may be written off. This means that it is removed, all or in part, from the balance sheet. This can have a significant impact on shareholders' equity, and may come as a surprise to investors. Writing off impaired assets is important, because the purpose of financial statements is to provide a fair and accurate depiction of the financial health of a company. This is why many investors calculate tangible book value in place of equity.

Bankruptcy

In cases of bankruptcy, creditors always come first, and so there may be nothing left for common shareholders (this is almost always the case if equity is negative).

What you will find on almost all company financial and news releases is a standard disclaimer about the uncertainty and risks related to forward-looking statements. Unfortunately, you will not always get a cautionary announcement from management when it comes to the company's ability to sustain operations. Executives may simply have the disclaimers in place and avoid communicating the risks in an open and transparent way to investors, unless they are challenged directly in a conference call—this is why it's important for shareholders to challenge management.

Bankruptcy announcements can really surprise investors who have not examined a company's financial health. It is not unusual for a conference call to be quite normal, or to have an extended period of no news, only to be followed by a bankruptcy announcement. Unprofitable operations might rely on financing to sustain day-to-day activities. If executives can't secure that financing, for whatever reason, the company is out of luck, and you may not receive very much warning if you haven't been paying attention. It is precisely for this reason that one must watch the cash balance of a company that is losing money.

Bankruptcy law comes in different flavors. For example, Chapter 11 bankruptcy means that a company is at risk of bankruptcy, but through debt and business reorganization it may reemerge successfully. However, for the most part, shareholders shouldn't come to expect much out of bankruptcy.

Qualitative Risks

Management

At the end of the day, people run companies. They come up with the ideas, control the assets, and follow through with operations. For this reason, it is always desirable to invest in companies with strong management. This isn't always an easy thing to assess. One of the ways that an investor can try to do this is to examine the history of senior executives. Were they able to successfully turn around failing businesses? Did they go bankrupt? Do they jump to a new company every few years? Were they former private equity owners—founders—of the company?

Stepping back for a moment, one very important question you might ask yourself is: Once the company raises capital, what further obligations and incentives does the company have toward shareholders? After all, once cash has been raised from the initial public offering, share price has no direct impact on the company itself. This is a bit of a trick question, but that doesn't make it any less important. There are both indirect and direct mechanisms at play, providing some of this obligation and incentive. Some of these mechanisms can also provide insight into the type of people running a company.

First, most companies will grant senior management the option to buy shares. This has two potential benefits. First, it is a form of noncash-based compensation. It allows a company to attract and pay individuals who have a rare and in-demand skillset without having to expend cash. Second, it provides an incentive. The executive is now not only earning a salary, but is a shareholder as well. By examining insider transactions (reported buy and sell orders), one can get some insight into the type of individual. If executives are selling a significant number of shares on an ongoing basis (unless those transactions are part of an automatic disposition plan), it may indicate that they have little interest in growing the company. They are looking to make some cash on the side at their convenience. They aren't *really* invested in the business. Conversely, insiders who acquire significant numbers of shares in the open market, with their own money, are without question shareholders. These individuals may be more interested in the company's operations, because the outcomes affect them more directly.

The second incentive is that they get paid to do their job, and to do it well. While senior executives are responsible for the direction of the business, they are not without oversight. The board of directors is responsible for ensuring that those executives are keeping the best interest of shareholders in mind. Note that one can also examine the previous experience of board members and their buy/sell activity just as one can with senior management.

Good management teams will make decisions that maximize shareholder value, and respond to market conditions accordingly. However, some executives may be committed to "business as usual," even if it is not in the interest of shareholders based on current market conditions. They might burn through shareholders' equity without any reservation as part of their day-to-day activities. It happens.

Finally, some companies can experience a high level of management turnover; new individuals might be hired and fired on a regular basis. This can set a company's operations back significantly. Different individuals can have very different visions for a company's direction. A new management team can have a very different strategy. Indeed, they may very well need to. However, it can take time and money to realize these strategies, especially for larger companies.

Economic Risks

Inflation

Inflation refers to the general increase in the price of goods and services over time, as the purchasing power of each unit of currency decreases. Inflation can occur when governments increase the money supply. This is an intentional tactic in some cases to reduce the relative debt owed by the country, since the dollar[28] amount of debt remains the same, but more dollars exist. This is sometimes the lesser of two evils, but generally something most people will want to avoid (especially savers).

In other cases, inflation is strictly the result of poor economic policy, which results in significant currency devaluation. At the height of Zimbabwe's hyperinflation in 2008, inflation was estimated to be 6.5 sextillion percent (10^{21}) in the month of November. 100 trillion dollar bills were printed and put into circulation. Ultimately Zimbabwe's

---

[28] The dollar is used in this example for illustrative purposes only.

national currency was abandoned in 2009, with foreign currencies being used for all transactions instead. There have been many more cases of hyperinflation.

This can be of concern to the investor who holds a significant amount of cash over a longer period of time. Investing in stocks can be a good hedge against inflation, because while the value of each dollar decreases, companies that provide goods and services should be collecting more dollars as well.

Deflation

Deflation occurs when the price of goods and services decreases over time, and so the purchasing power of each unit of currency actually increases. In this case, one does not want to be holding debt, since the absolute dollar amount of debt remains fixed, while incomes will usually drop.

Deflation can occur as a result of decreasing demand for goods and services. In order to compete, businesses are forced to lower prices, and so they may be forced to lower their costs, meaning that many companies in the manufacturing and service chain must also lay off staff and decrease wages. Central banks can try to compensate for deflation by increasing the money supply or by lowering interest rates in order to encourage borrowing, spending, and investing—something they will probably do at all costs.

For *investors*, deflation is a greater risk than inflation. Whereas in the case of inflation some businesses will simply be earning more dollars, effectively compensating for the loss in purchasing power per dollar, deflation results in lower earnings, lower margins, and lower profits, resulting in lower cash flow and lower share prices.

Geopolitical Risks

Forced Nationalization

Every company must abide by the laws of the country in which it operates. Some countries are friendlier than others when it comes to free markets and capitalism.

In some extreme instances, there have been cases of *forced* nationalization, often during regime changes. This is where a government seizes the assets of a business on the grounds that it can, effectively taking control of the equity that used to belong to shareholders. This is a risk that investors take when they invest in some politically unstable places.

Investors should be aware of where the companies they invest in operate, or are thinking of operating in the future, and whether governments there are friendly to business or not.

Regional Conflict

Unfortunately, war and conflict are still very much a part of the world today. Many of these regions are rich in resources, and therefore attractive to mining companies, for better or for worse. Should a conflict arise in a region where a company operates, it is a good idea to follow the news, check where it is operating on a map relative to the known areas of conflict, and understand the nature of the conflict.

Many of these countries are quite large, and whether a company's operations are affected or not can depend on where it is located relative to the regional areas of infighting (it is not unusual for some parts of a country to be in conflict while others remain defended and stable). Depending on where the company's operations are located, operations may need to be ceased and personnel evacuated for an unknown, perhaps indefinite, period of time.

Local Unrest

Sometimes the local population will protest against a company project. Sometimes this is for very legitimate reasons (environmental concerns, etc.). In very poor areas, where mines are often developed, the local governments usually require the operating company to contribute to the local area (building schools, etc.) and hire some of the local population. Even then, the local population might protest, sometimes violently, which can result in operations being halted for an uncertain period of time.

Securities Fraud

Stock-Manipulation Schemes

As an investor, you need to be aware of the existence of certain forms of fraud that can occur. One of the most common examples of fraud that an investor might encounter is called a "pump and dump" scheme, and it can exist on a number of different scales. In this case, somebody purchases shares in a company that may or may not have any value ("penny stocks" are a common choice because they typically trade at lower volumes, and so the price can be manipulated more easily with only a few trades). The fraudsters will then promote this stock, sometimes by making false claims through online forums in an effort to drive demand for the stock, with the intent to sell once enough investors get on board. This is completely illegal, and people have been prosecuted for it.

Financial Deception and Fraud

While it is the job of senior management and the board of directors to accurately report a company's financial results, there have been some very serious cases of financial deception and fraud. Two clear examples are Enron and Bre-X.

Enron was an American energy-trading company, and at one point was one of the largest companies in the United States. It was found to be falsely reporting its revenues through misleading accounting practices. When the fraud was revealed, the company's share price dropped from more than $80 to less than $0.50, and the company eventually went bankrupt in 2001, leaving shareholders with nothing. Many individuals who were invested in Enron lost a significant amount of money, simply because they were given falsified financial reports.

Bre-X Minerals was a Canadian gold miner in Indonesia that falsely reported that it had found significant amounts of gold on one of its properties. When it was revealed that there was in fact very little gold at all, the share price dropped from more than $250 to mere pennies. In 2002 Bre-X went bankrupt, and it is known as one of the biggest mining frauds in history.

Short-Sale Market Flooding

While it is not this book's intent to suggest that any institutions are actually guilty of this practice, an investor should be aware of the risk of market manipulation. Most large firms will have access to market-depth information, including where other investors have placed sell orders that will be triggered should the stock drop below a certain price. A large enough firm, with sufficient capital, might flood the market with a significant number of short-sale orders (selling borrowed stocks, which must be purchased back at a lower price to make a profit), thereby triggering a chain of automatic sell orders and/or margin calls if there is not enough buying volume. The company may then be able to cover (buy back to close their short position) as this selling takes place at a much lower price in order to make money (perhaps by buying into a larger volume sell order that has been triggered).

Normal short selling would not be able to move the price so significantly, but large investors do have the ability to really move stock prices, because of the sheer volume of shares they are able to buy and sell. While this is an illegal practice, investors should be aware that it can occur.

Price Risks

Low-Volume Stocks

Sometimes only a few shares of a stock will trade on a given day. Sometimes no shares of stock will trade for days on end. This can make it difficult to liquidate your position should you need to, and can result in significant changes to share price based on only a small number of shares, because of the limited market depth.

At the same time, if investors become more interested in a company, daily trading volumes can increase significantly.

Panic Selling

Investors are people, and people have emotions. When it comes to money, people can have strong feelings, whether they are rational or not. If the price of a stock is dropping, many people will sell out of fear or for their peace of mind—*especially* if they didn't understand what they were buying in the first place. Sometimes this is the right decision, and sometimes it isn't. In either case, panic does result in selling. Never assume that all investors are rational. To be fair, we all make mistakes. If a stock has only a limited market depth, it may take only a few people to panic for the stock to drop significantly in price.

Margin Calls

Some investors and funds make use of leverage (borrowed money) in order to try and improve their returns, by increasing the number of shares that they control. While this can provide a higher return, it also exposes them to a greater risk. If the share price drops enough, or the market is flooded with short sales and there aren't enough buyers, lenders can force those investors to liquidate their positions in order to recover the borrowed money (leaving the investor with nothing). This can cause further declines in price as a result of automatic selling, whether the investors wanted to sell or not. This is one of the reasons why you should always invest with your own money, and never somebody else's.

Stock Market Crashes

Stock market crashes can occur for a variety of reasons. Quite often they are proceeded by serious economic events. If you have invested in companies with lower speculative premiums, solid margins, and reliable cash flow, you should be less worried. People who don't understand the link between stocks and companies will certainly be afraid of "stock market crashes" no matter what.

When markets crash, quite often larger players will simply liquidate many of their holdings across the board, in an effort to "sell before the price drops even further"; this is an unfortunate reality, based more on gaming market price than actually buying and holding good stocks that should provide a solid return over time. Some mutual funds may be forced to sell large blocks of shares as units are sold back to the fund and redeemed. For the investor, this is still a price risk. For those who have not invested, it may represent an opportunity.

Stocks will almost always crash the hardest when speculative premiums are the highest.

Investing Principles

- It is important to familiarize yourself not only with the financial red flags that you may find on a company's current financial statements, but also with those risks that can occur in the future — financial or otherwise.

- Bankruptcy is rarely announced ahead of time. You need to understand a company's financial health.

- People run companies. Quite often the best people to run companies are shareholders as well (especially if they invested in those shares on the open market, or participated in stock offerings).

- While neither is desirable, for the most part deflation is a greater risk to investors than inflation.

- Forced nationalization, regional conflict, and local unrest are all geopolitical risks that can affect a company's ability to operate.

- While they are illegal, cases of securities fraud do persist, and shareholders pay for it. Even very large companies have been found guilty of fraud. This is a risk most investors cannot control for.

- Stock price can change for reasons beyond a company's financial position. Stocks that trade at lower volumes are more susceptible to large changes in price, based on only a limited number of trades.

7

Investing in Funds

For many people, it makes sense to invest in diversified funds that hold a number of assets, rather than picking individual stocks. Others prefer funds to form the backbone of their investments, while allocating only a small portion of their investment capital to specific stocks. Even if you are capable of picking individual stocks, the discipline of contributing regularly to a fund should not be underestimated. Your contributions can really add up over the long term.

One of the biggest advantages to investing in funds is that you expose yourself to the same risk as the general market (assuming you are invested in a fund that tracks the general market), and so if the market crashes, your losses will be roughly in line with those of most other people, and not significantly worse.

While funds offer a more hands-off approach to investing, it is still important to understand what you are buying. A fund's unit price is directly related to the price of its underlying assets, which may be overvalued or undervalued, and so diversification aside, you are still subject to some of the same risks as holding stocks. The exception is when the fund you are invested in holds lower-volatility assets, like bonds, or stocks that generate regular and predictable income in the form of dividends.

Like stocks, few people understand the link between fund units, and their underlying holdings—how those units are created.

Mutual Funds

Mutual funds are professionally managed funds where each unit in that fund entitles the holder to a stake in a basket of underlying companies and/or other securities (including stocks and bonds). Different mutual funds will have different risk profiles, depending on the type of securities they invest in.

Mutual funds are an incredibly popular financial instrument because they offer simplicity, diversification, and a way to invest in broader markets and sectors without having to investigate and pick individual stocks. This is also a risk, because the investor is, to some degree, assuming price represents fair value, which may not be the case. The only thing you can be assured of is that the unit price is tied to the prices of its underlying assets, not that those assets are valued by the markets correctly.

There are two types of mutual funds: "open-end" and "closed-end" funds, which are classified based on the way in which units are created. While mutual funds are hands-off and professionally managed, they are not completely opaque. Most funds will list their top holdings, including specific stocks and asset classes. This allows an investor to identify and examine the underlying holdings, to some extent. Otherwise, most investors will only see the historical returns (or losses) that the fund has provided each year.

Closed-End Funds

The first mutual funds were closed-end funds. In a closed-end fund, a fixed number of units are created when the fund is introduced, and sold to investors. This is similar to an IPO, except that no new units will be created after the initial offering. The money raised when those units are sold to investors is then invested in underlying stocks or securities, which are subject to change based on the fund manager's decisions (this is what fund managers are paid for). In this sense, one could even think of a closed-end fund as a company that invests in other companies (and securities).

These units can then be traded *between* investors throughout the day, just like a stock. While the unit price should be approximately equal to the net asset value (NAV), which is really just the weighted price of the underlying securities per unit, it will vary based on what investors are willing to buy or sell for. The difference between unit price and NAV can vary considerably in a closed-end fund.

Open-End Funds

In an open-end fund, there is no limit to the number of units that can exist. Units are "created" and "destroyed" in blocks when they are bought or sold to meet investor demand. Unlike a closed-end fund, units are *not* traded between investors, but rather bought from, and sold to, the company that operates the fund directly. When there is enough demand, the underlying shares will be purchased in blocks to create more units. When units are sold by investors, they are "redeemed," in that the fund is said to "buy back" those units, where the underlying stocks may eventually be sold back to the stock market in blocks.

Units of an open-end fund do not trade throughout the day on an exchange like a closed-end fund. Instead, their value is updated once and only once at the end of the day based on the NAV, less management fees. Most mutual funds are open-ended funds, which are generally considered to be better investment vehicles than closed-end funds for most investors. Just like closed-end funds, fund managers may decide to change the composition of the underlying holdings over time in an effort to achieve the best fund performance.

Management Fees

Note that you will be required to pay a fee, called the management expense ratio (MER), if you invest in mutual funds. This is how the company that issues the fund makes money, and how it pays the fund managers who run it. For example, if you were to invest in a fund with an MER of two percent, which returns five percent in a year, your actual return would be three percent. This fee varies from fund to fund. Note that some mutual funds invest in a very similar way to exchange-traded funds, in some cases having nearly identical holdings—especially in the case where they seek to track a particular index (usually the weighted average of a known group of stocks, used as a measure of all or part of the market). In this case, investing directly in an exchange-traded fund is probably a better idea, because the management fee will usually be much lower.

It is important to understand that the companies that manage open-end funds will also make money by growing the size of the fund — by issuing more units. They take a percent of the fund each year, whether it provides a return to investors or not. Of course, if the fund doesn't perform, investors are likely to pull their money out of it.

Exchange-Traded Funds

Exchange-traded funds (ETFs) differ from mutual funds in that they tend to be less actively managed, often tracking indices instead. As a result, they will usually have a lower MER. Like closed-end funds, ETFs trade like a stock, and so the unit price can change throughout the day.

Units of an ETF are created differently than those of a mutual fund. We will limit our discussion to the impact this difference has, rather than the specific details. Some market participants are able to take advantage of something called arbitrage, when the unit price of an ETF deviates too far from its NAV. Arbitrage involves profiting from this difference in prices between multiple markets. This mechanism prevents the price of each unit in an ETF from diverging too far from the underlying NAV, which is one of the possible risks associated with closed-end funds. This means that the price you pay for each unit, throughout the day, tends to reflect the price of the underlying securities. If you are investing to track an index, an ETF is probably your best bet.

Investing Principles

- Mutual funds and ETFs provide a simple and diversified way of investing in a basket of underlying securities.

- Mutual funds are professionally managed and typically have a higher management fee than ETFs.

- In a closed-end fund, a fixed number of units are issued, and are traded between investors throughout the day. The unit price can deviate quite a lot from the NAV in a closed-end fund.

- In an open-end fund, units are created and redeemed based on investor demand. Units do not trade on an exchange, and the price is updated at the end of each day based on the NAV. Most mutual funds are open-end funds, and most investors who wish to invest in a mutual fund should probably invest in open-end funds.

- ETFs trade like closed-end funds on an exchange, but their unit price tracks NAV more closely as a result of arbitrage. ETFs generally track indices for a lower MER than mutual funds.

8
Buy and Sell Orders

In order to buy and sell shares, it is necessary to open an investing account with a brokerage firm or your bank. You can expect a modest transaction fee for every buy and sell order that the firm or bank executes on your behalf. This fee can vary depending on the company you use. If you are purchasing only small quantities of shares, it is important to factor these fees into your overall investment cost. Buying and selling a lot of shares in a relatively short period of time can cost quite a bit of money, and those transactions are easily overlooked.

It is important to realize that you may not necessarily be able to buy or sell shares at the last stock price.[29] For every transaction, there is only a limited quantity of shares; each bid and ask order is finite in volume. There is actually a distribution of buy and sell orders at different prices and

---

[29] Note that the latest stock price is often delayed by fifteen minutes or so, depending on your source of market data, and so you may be unable to fulfill an order at that price should the stock price change.

volumes above and below the last market price—the market depth. There may even be a gap between the current bid and ask price, should there be only a few buyers and sellers. This distribution is constantly changing. While you will typically only see the last share price, along with the current bid and ask prices (and the volume of shares available at each), it is possible to subscribe to the underlying market depth[30] for a fee.

There are two main types of orders that you can place when you buy or sell: market orders and limit orders.

Market Orders

A market order is the simplest type of order you can place. However, it is recommended that you do *not* make use of this type of order. When you place a market order, you specify only a volume of shares that you wish to buy or sell, and not a price. The order for that volume of shares will be fulfilled immediately, but you may end up paying more or selling for less than you would like.

When you buy using a market order your order will be fulfilled by purchasing shares at the lowest asking price that sellers are asking. However, if there aren't enough shares available at that price to fulfill your entire order, the order will also purchase available shares above that price until your order is complete. If there are a lot of shares available at or around the current market price, you will probably pay no

---

[30] Subscribing to market-depth information will be of little benefit to most investors. However, it can be an interesting exercise to see where large buy and sell orders exist relative to the current share price.

more than the most recent market price. However, if there are only a handful of sell orders near the current market price, you may end up having your order filled at a much higher price than you had hoped.

Similarly, if you were to sell using a market order, you may not be able to sell all of your shares at the highest bid price, because there may not be enough buyers. Instead, you may end up selling to buyers at much lower prices in order to fill your entire market order.

For this reason, it is often unwise to try to sell large quantities of shares at once. With many institutions using software and algorithms to run their trading automatically (as silly as this may be), this bid/ask distribution can change quickly as orders are placed, filled, or cancelled at high speed. As an investor, you shouldn't allow such distributions to concern you too much, as you cannot predict how they will change, but it is useful to understand that they exist.

Limit Orders

Most investors should be placing limit orders all the time. In this case, you specify not only the quantity of shares that you would like to buy or sell, but also a price. This price is the limit price. You may also specify a date at which the unfulfilled part of the order will expire. A limit order can remain open for days, or even weeks, should you choose. You can also cancel the unfulfilled portion of a limit order at any time (you may wish to place a new order at a new limit price). The benefit to placing a limit order is that you can be sure that you will not buy shares for more than, or sell shares for less than, the limit price. The caveat is that your order might be fulfilled only in part, or not at all, should you set the limit price too high or too low.

When you buy using a limit order, you specify a price at or below which your order will be filled should shares be available at those prices on the market. Your order will be partially filled as shares become available in that range, until it is complete or you cancel the rest of your order. The risk is that the share price may never drop to or below the limit price, and so your order might never be filled. If you really want your order to be filled, you may try bidding with a limit price just at or above the current ask price, guaranteeing that you won't pay more per share than you specify as your limit price. Others choose a limit price that is below the current market price, with the hope to fill the order should the market price drop before the order expires.

When you sell using a limit order, you specify a price at or above which your order will be filled should buyers be willing to pay those prices for shares. This guarantees that you will not sell at a price lower than you would like. The risk is that your order may not be filled should buyers be unwilling to purchase shares at or above the limit price before the order expires. Again, if you really want your order to be filled, you may try selling with a limit price just below the current market price.

Stop-Limit Orders

A stop-limit order is a special type of limit order that you can place that requires you to specify a stop price as well.

When the current market price hits the stop price, your stop-limit order automatically becomes a limit order. Like all limit orders, you can also specify a date at which the unfulfilled part of the order will expire.

While you can place a stop-limit buy order, it is generally less useful than a stop-limit sell order. A stop-limit sell order is an automatic way of protecting your gains or limiting your losses should the stock price drop suddenly. In this case, you specify a stop price below the current market price, with a limit price somewhere below the stop price. Should the stop price be reached, a sell-limit order is automatically placed, where your broker will try to sell all or part of your order at or above the limit price. If the stock price drops below the limit price before your order is completely fulfilled, no more shares will be sold until more buyers make offers above the limit price (just like a normal sell-limit order, the limit price sets the lowest price you are willing to sell shares at).

There is a risk that the stock could drop just below your stop price to trigger your stop-limit order, and then quickly rebound, in which case you may be selling at a bad time. You can usually subscribe to an e-mail alert that tells you when the stock drops to a certain price. You may wish to set such an alert at, or perhaps above, your stop price so that you are aware that such an event has taken place and you can act accordingly by cancelling your stop-limit order if you do not wish to sell.

Stop-limit orders are a little bit more complex than limit orders, and so their use should be investigated further if you are interested. Most investors probably won't need to use this type of order, but some might find it valuable.

Investing Principles

- The market depth consists of all current buy and sell orders above and below the current market price. For every bid/ask order, there are only a finite number of shares at any given time.

- Market orders are subject to the risk of being filled at unexpected and undesirable prices should there be a limited number of buyers or sellers. Most investors should not use market orders. This is especially true when buying or selling shares in a company with low trading volume.

- Limit orders ensure that you buy shares at or below the limit price, and sell shares at or above the limit price, should buyers or sellers be available at those prices. Most investors should use limit orders.

- Stop-limit orders become limit orders once the stop price is reached. This is sometimes used to automatically sell your shares, should the stock drop below the stop price.

- A date can be specified for all limit orders. The unfulfilled part of a limit order will expire on that date.

- Always be careful when placing buy and sell orders—double check the price(s) and volume you set before placing the order.

Investing Checklist

Every investment is unique, and depends on a number of different variables under circumstances that are subject to change. Therefore, an investor needs to develop his or her own process for assessing those variables in order to establish value, and to understand the risks involved. The following list is just one example of such a process. Many experienced investors have an internal checklist of items. To be rigorous, you should write your own list, editing and expanding on the one below—what are your criteria?

1. **What's the market capitalization of the company? You need to decide if the company is undervalued or overvalued relative to that price.[31]**

2. **Check the balance sheet to understand the company's current financial health and valuation.**

    - Equity—is there any? How much is tangible? Are retained earnings positive?
    - P/B—what's the market premium (or discount) on tangible book value?
    - Liquidity—does the company have sufficient current assets to cover its current liabilities?
    - Asset composition—what does the company own? How much is cash, inventory, property?

---

[31] Some investors will try to determine the fair value of a company first, and look at the market capitalization last (they estimate what they would be willing to pay before looking at what the market is offering).

- Debt—is there a lot on the books? Can the company service it?

3. **Check the income statement to determine the company's previous profitability.**

    - Revenue—does the company have any? Is it growing?
    - Gross profit margin—is there one? How big is it?
    - Net profit margin—is the company profitable? By how much?
    - P/E—what's the market price relative to earnings?
    - Unusual items—are there any one-time occurrences resulting in a higher-than-usual net income or net loss?
    - Dividends—are they sustainable; is the company paying out more than it makes through operations?

4. **Check the cash flow statement to understand how cash has been generated or consumed.**

    - Cash from operations—is cash flow positive? Is it more, or less than net income? Why?
    - Cash from investing activities—is the company investing a significant amount of capital?
    - Cash from financing activities—is the company raising cash; what's the source of that cash?
    - Net change in cash—is the company losing cash? Is it being lost because of operations, or is it being invested wisely? If it is raising cash, is it from operations, equity, or debt issues?

5. Resource Company Property Assets (if applicable)

- Research the company's properties—what are its proven and probable reserves; what are the resource grades?
- Examine expected capital expenditures—can the company finance these? Will it need to issue shares?
- Projected operating costs—how much does it cost the company to extract the resource? What does the resource price need to be for the company to make a profit?
- What are the company's expected annual production levels?
- What's the current resource price, its historical volatility, and the macroeconomic factors that influence it?
- Feasibility—has the company put together a study from technical reports? What's the projected NPV and IRR for the property? What are its expected cash flows and at what resource price? What's the payback period?
- Are its properties worth more than the listed value on its balance sheet?

6. Review qualitative company information, website, etc.

- What does the company do? What do they sell? What's the vision?
- Examine risk factors (management, geopolitical, etc.)

7. Compare to other companies in the industry.

- Are there better investment opportunities?

- Is anybody profiting in this industry — maybe it's not a good sector to be in?

8. **Examine insider transactions for unusual activity.**

   - Are insiders buying or selling shares on the public market? Is it more than usual?

9. **Set price and news alerts.**

10. **Follow quarterly financial releases and company news.**

    - Is it time to sell (at a profit or loss?)
    - Are there any material changes in the company's operations that could affect future profitability?

11. **Place a stop-limit sell order (if desired, and the stock is sufficiently liquid).**

Glossary

Accrual Accounting: A common method of accounting where income and expenses are recorded at the time of sale, but not necessarily when the cash is actually collected or paid.

Accumulated Depreciation: The total depreciation of a tangible asset up to the current point in time; the difference between the purchase price of an asset and its current value.

Assets: Economic resources that are controlled but not necessarily owned by a company and have or are capable of producing value. These can be tangible, such as cash, accounts receivable, property, and equipment, or intangible, such as goodwill, patents, or trademarks.

Ask Price: The lowest price that an investor is willing to sell shares for; it is normally associated with some volume of shares at that price.

Balance Sheet: A financial statement that discloses a company's assets, liabilities, and equity as of a specific date.

Bid Price: The highest price an investor is willing to buy shares for; this is normally associated with some volume of shares at that price.

Cash Flow Statement: A financial statement that discloses the sources, uses and the change in a company's cash over a period of time; broken down into operating, investing, and financing activities.

Depreciation: The process of deducting value from the purchase price of a tangible asset over the course of its useful and expected life; this is considered a noncash expense.

EPS: Earnings per share; calculated as net income minus dividends, divided by the current number of common shares.

***Diluted* EPS:** EPS calculated by using the total number of shares should all outstanding options and warrants be exercised.

Equity: The portion of a company's assets that is owned by shareholders; this is calculated as the difference between total assets and total liabilities.

GAAP: Generally Accepted Accounting Principles; a common method of accounting in the United States.

Goodwill: An intangible asset that represents the difference between the cash paid for an acquisition and its equity.

Income Statement: A financial statement that provides information about a company's earnings and profitability over the reporting period.

Initial Public Offering (IPO): A process by which a private company transforms into a public company by issuing shares of its stock for the first time directly to the public (qualifying investors, usually of some minimum net worth) in exchange for cash.

IFRS: International Financial Reporting Standard; a common method of accounting that most countries have or are adopting.

Intangibles: Nonphysical assets that may have value, such as goodwill and patents.

Leverage: The use of debt to increase the assets controlled by a company, usually in an effort to increase returns.

Liabilities: The portion of a company's assets that is owned to creditors, requiring settlement over time.

Liquidity: *(Accounting)* The ability to meet short-term debts and obligations. A company with poor liquidity may be forced to enter bankruptcy. *(Markets)* The ease with which one is able to buy or sell shares without significantly affecting the price, based on the number of buyers and sellers.

Market Capitalization: A measure of the market valuation of a publicly traded company, calculated as the number of shares outstanding times the current share price.

Net Present Value: The current value of a company or project based on the present value of all future cash inflows and outflows that it would generate or consume over time; important for estimating the value of complex projects.

Payables: Money owed by the company within a short period of time, usually one year; a current liability.

Receivables: Money owed to the company within a short period of time, usually one year; a current asset.

Retained Earnings: Accumulated net income that has not been paid out as dividends; on a balance sheet, this represents the change in shareholders' equity through operations.

Revenue: The dollar amount the company receives, usually from the sale of good or services to customers, before expenses, through regular business operations over an accounting period.

Solvency: The ability to meet long-term debts and obligations.

Tangible Book Value: Calculated as equity less intangible assets (including goodwill). This is a more conservative estimate of liquidation value, because it assumes intangible assets have no value.

Working Capital: A measure of liquidity; this is calculated as the difference between current assets and current liabilities.

Resources

Stock Quotes, Financial Statements, and News

Google Finance
www.google.com/finance

Yahoo Finance
finance.yahoo.com

Detailed Filings and Insider Activity

United States Securities and Exchange Commission (SEC)
Electronic Data Gathering, Analysis, and Retrieval system
(EDGAR)
www.sec.gov/edgar.shtml

Canadian Securities Administrators (CSA) System for
Electronic Document Analysis and Retrieval (SEDAR)
www.sedar.com

Canadian Securities Administrators (CSA) System for
Electronic Disclosure by Insiders (SEDI)
www.sedi.ca

Insider Tracking—easy to navigate, provides most recent
insider transactions for free, or full reports for a fee
www.insidertracking.com

Stock Screeners

Google Finance Stock Screener
www.google.com/finance#stockscreener

News Alerts

Google Alerts—useful for setting email news alerts for companies
www.google.com/alerts

Economic Research

World Bank Data—detailed global economic and development indicators
data.worldbank.org

Federal Reserve Economic Research and Data
www.federalreserve.gov/econresdata

General Business and Financial News[*]

Bloomberg
www.bloomberg.com

The Wall Street Journal
online.wsj.com

The Economist
www.economist.com

---

[*] When it comes to investing information and financial advice, question everything you read.

Where do you go from here?

Practice reading and evaluating financial statements. Determine the premium (or discount) that you pay for equity today. What are the risks? What's the value for shareholders in the future?

If you haven't already, one of the best things that you can do is take an introductory college or continuing education course on basic financial analysis. Where you are unsure, consider asking the advice of an investment professional.

To provide feedback on this first edition, to ask any questions, or to inquire about the Education Program, which provides paperback copies at a discount to schools, courses, and student clubs, please visit

www.principlesofinvestingbook.com

Printed in Great Britain
by Amazon